Associated Press

Sports Writing Handbook

Steve Wilstein

McGraw-Hill

New York   Chicago   San Francisco   Lisbon
London   Madrid   Mexico City   Milan   New Delhi
San Juan   Seoul   Singapore   Sydney   Toronto

McGraw-Hill

A Division of The McGraw·Hill Companies

1 2 3 4 5 6 7 8 9 0   DOC/DOC   0 9 8 7 6 5 4 3 2 1

ISBN 0-07-137218-0

This book was set in Stempel Garamond by North Market Street Graphics.

Printed and bound by R. R. Donnelley & Sons Company.

This publication is designed to provide accurate and authoritative information in regard to the subject matter covered. It is sold with the understanding that the publisher is not engaged in rendering legal, accounting, or other professional service. If legal advice or other expert assistance is required, the services of a competent professional person should be sought.
                    —From a declaration of principles adopted by a committee of the
                    American Bar Association and a committee of publishers.

 This book is printed on recycled, acid-free paper containing a minimum of 50% recycled de-inked fibers.

McGraw-Hill book are available at special quantity discounts to use as premiums and sales promotions or for use in corporate training programs. For more information, please write to the Director of Special Sales, Professional Publishing, McGraw-Hill, Two Penn Plaza, New York, NY 10121-2298. Or contact your local bookstore.

This book is dedicated to my daughter, Tara, who is blessed with her mother's beauty and brains. She grew up while I chased stories and missed some of her birthdays, yet she still loves to go with her dad every summer on busman's holidays at the ballpark.

Contents

Acknowledgments

Thanks are due to Norm Goldstein at The Associated Press, who shepherded this book from start to finish. He proposed the idea and persisted even after I ignored his first two entreaties because I was too busy covering sports to write about how to do it. Also to Paula Froke, the kind of editor who is a writer's best ally, for squeezing in the time to edit the first draft with a keen eye and a feathery touch between crises on the AP's General Desk.

Thanks, too, to AP sports editor Terry Taylor, who has never minded my midnight phone calls or the line I usually give her when I finish a feature: It's a little longer than you wanted. I am indebted to the many colleagues I've worked with at events over the years who have shared laughs and stories, sometimes at late-night dinners just before the last restaurant in town closes.

I am particularly grateful to those who gave me their time and insights for this book: Neil Amdur, Dave Anderson, Ira Berkow, Christine Brennan, Bill Dwyre, Jim Litke, Bob Ryan, George Vecsey, and Michael Wilbon. That's a tough lineup to beat.

Most of all I am thankful for my lovely Chris, who hides out with me in the woods and trips with me through the city, making life fun while I punch out the pages.

—Steve Wilstein

Introduction

Make it sing, sports writers tell each other as they sit hunched over their laptops in cramped press boxes and tents. And the refrain often comes back that they will be lucky to make it hum a few bars. But the idea is always there, to take a scene, a game, an interview and make the story sing and the words dance off the page. The best writers, masters of the storytelling art, do it day after day for decades.

They watch for those moments that make each game different from all the others, tune in on the fresh, taut, witty quotes that snap the characters to life on the page, search for the color and detail that make it all feel real.

The sports writers' challenge is to describe events with elegance and passion and wit, to make readers share their laughter or tears or rage, to entertain and inform, to break the news that no one else knows or describe a game that everyone has seen, to impart a feeling for what it was like to be there in the stands or on the field or in the locker room, to give the event meaning and put it in perspective. Oh, and the deadline is in 15 minutes.

Muhammad Ali watches as the flame rises to the Olympic torch during the opening ceremonies of the 1996 Summer Olympic Games on Friday, July 19, 1996, in Atlanta. (AP Photo/Doug Mills)

Photographers surround the U.S. men's 4 × 100 meter relay team after they won the gold medal at the Summer Olympics, Saturday, Sept. 30, 2000, at Olympic Stadium in Sydney. (AP Photo/ Michael Probst)

The intent of this book is to give prospective sports writers an understanding of the real world of covering sports, what it takes to do the job every day, working weekends and holidays, in heat and cold, sunshine and snow, always under the pressure of deadlines. The late great Red Smith once said sports writing is easy, you just open a vein and let your blood drip on the page. Smith had a genius for irony and understatement. Sometimes you wish you could get off that easily.

Nobody cares how much effort it takes or what you have to do to get the story in, just as long as you do. Over the years, I have filed from a bait and tackle shop on a mountain, a broom closet outside a John Elway news conference, under the ring at a Muhammad Ali fight. At the Australian Open a few years ago, when the newsroom was flooded ankle deep by a backed-up drain, the *Boston Globe*'s Bud Collins calmly took off his shoes and socks, set his chair up on top of his desk, and kept typing with his laptop on his lap high above the water. He was on deadline.

We're all still looking for the magical story that writes itself. At a big event, the more obvious the lead, it seems, the harder it is to get right, to convey the magnitude of the moment, to weave in the elements that made it happen, to place it into historical context, and to assess the impact it will have on the future of the athlete, the sport, the fans. When you do, when the words match the moment and you know you've nailed it, nothing feels better. When you don't, you toss sleeplessly in strange hotel rooms, thinking of all the lines you should have written and fighting the urge to stomp on your laptop until it dies.

Sports writing is much less about sports than it is about writing. It's not about being a super-fan, memorizing a million statistics, and rhapsodizing or ranting in print about how awesome or awful the game was. In

AP Iowa sports editor Chuck Schoffner covers an Iowa State women's basketball game at the University of Northern Iowa in Cedar Falls. (AP Photo by Charlie Neibergall)

fact, the day you become a sports writer is the day you stop acting like a fan, even if you never lose the fan's passion that drew you into sports and keeps you going. You don't cheer in the press box or ask for autographs in the club-house. You don't wear the name of your favorite team on your shirt or the number of your favorite athlete on your back. You don't worship ballplayers or turn them into gods. You have the kind of access that fans dream about, and it's your job to bring them silently along with you, to let them see and hear what's going on as if they were by your side.

Nothing beats legwork—going to the games and practices, talking to the athletes and coaches and everyone around them, filling notebooks with a million details that might never get used, finding the gems that will make the story sparkle. Good sports writing is good, honest reporting, not relying on play-by-play descriptions handed out moments after a game or quote sheets filled with banal

Chicago Bulls' Michael Jordan is the center of attention as he talks with reporters at the teams training facility in Deerfield, Ill., in this March 20, 1995, photo. (AP Photo/Robert Kozloff)

St. Louis Cardinals slugger Mark McGwire gives a scowl as he is surrounded by media before playing against the Chicago Cubs on Monday, Aug. 18, 1998 in Chicago. The closer McGwire gets to breaking the single-season home run record, the greater the media interest has become. (AP Photo/John Gaps III)

comments about executing and being focused. It's about watching events in person, listening to the sounds of the crowd, smelling the air and feeling the temperature, not lazily watching on television at the office or in a windowless press room. It's about breaking from the herd and searching for something unique and unexpected. It's about being original and clever, passionate and true,

not just going through the motions to fill space in the paper.

Whether you're writing for *The New York Times* or *The Arlington Times,* covering the Super Bowl or a high school game, the World Series or Little League, the opportunity is there to tell the story with eloquence and excitement and make it sing for the readers. No sports writer goes straight from college to cover Wimbledon.

Italy's goalie Luca Marchegiani lies on the grass after Mexico's Marcelino Bernal, left of ball, blasted the ball into the net during the Italy and Mexico Group E World Cup match, Tuesday, June 28, 1994, at Washington's RFK Stadium. Italy and Mexico tied 1-1 and Mexico will advance to the next round. (AP Photo/Doug Mills)

No one begins by interviewing Shaquille O'Neal in the NBA Playoffs. Writers get there by putting in the effort on hundreds of smaller stories, sharpening their skills, broadening their background, developing their judgment, proving they can handle the big assignments and deserve them. Every word, every sentence, every story in a writer's life counts. So does spelling.

I begin this book at the end of a typically busy year of covering sports, rambling from event to event as the seasons slipped seamlessly one into the other. It was a year, like most of my past 30, when many of the aspects of the sports writing craft were called into play: beat reporting; filing fast on deadline; writing columns, features, and enterprise packages; covering meetings and court hearings; explaining medical and legal issues; editing other writers; cramming to cover Olympic sports we see only once every four years.

It was a year when I wrote about a quarter-million words, flew about 100,000 miles, and stayed more than 200 nights in hotels . . . another year when I left pens, a tape recorder, an organizer, sunglasses, odd socks, and taxi receipts scattered on three continents. There were many memorable moments—Bob Knight getting fired at Indiana, Venus Williams and Pete Sampras winning Wimbledon, Marion Jones running wild at the Olympics, the Yankees beating the Mets in the Subway Series, Darryl Strawberry standing shackled before a judge in a Florida courtroom—and hundreds of forgettable ones.

People often ask, only half jokingly, if they can carry my bag when they hear I'm off to the Olympics or the Super Bowl or the World Series. Friends who are lawyers or doctors or executives wish they could trade jobs. Heck, even Richard Nixon once said that, all things considered, he'd rather have been a sports writer. And he and the country might have been much better off if he had.

Being a sports writer seems such an easy life. Surely it beats real work—there's no heavy lifting and you can often sleep late. Good writers also can make a pretty decent living and earn a fair amount of fame, even if they never become as rich or famous as the people they write about. Red Smith might have sweated blood over his column, but he knew exactly how good his gig was. "Sports writing," he contended, "is the most pleasant way of making a living which man has yet devised."

Yet it's not for everyone. There are constant deadlines, endless flights and cabs to catch, days spent on the road away from the family and nights spent alone in hotel rooms, eating room-service meals while punching out another story. Not everyone has the skills to do it well or the willingness to make the sacrifices the sporting life requires. But if you have the ability and the desire to be a sports writer, if it's in your bones the way the stage is for actors, then let us explore what it takes to succeed by listening to advice from some of the best in the business.

The emphasis in this book is less on telling tales of the road or the big events than it is on know-

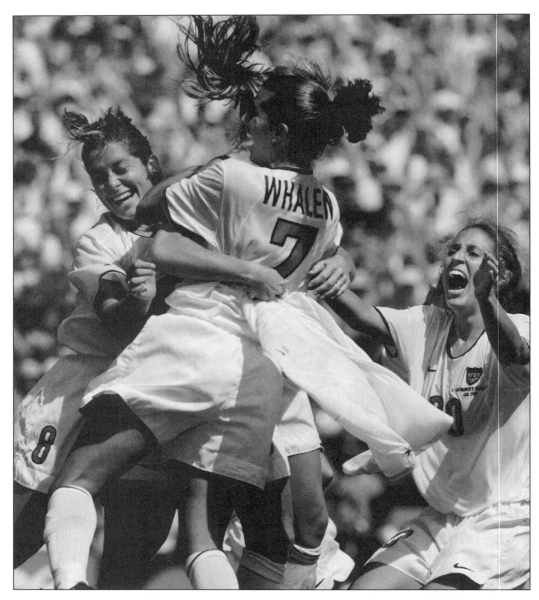

The United States' Brandi Chastain, center, is greeted by teammates Shannon MacMillan (8), Sara Whalen (7), and Kate Sobrero (20) after kicking the game-winning overtime penalty shootout kick against China during the Women's World Cup Final at the Rose Bowl in Pasadena, Calif., Saturday, July 10, 1999. The U.S. won the shootout 5-4 after the game ended in a 0-0 tie. (AP Photo/Mark J. Terrill)

ing what to do when you get there. We will look at sports writing as it is done, or should be done, daily at The Associated Press and in newspapers and magazines and on the Internet. That's different in many ways from the sports writing of John Updike, Thomas McGuane, Roger Angell, and many other notable writers whose work often appears in sports anthologies. There's no question that those writers tell marvelous stories—Updike's essay on Ted Williams, "Hub Fans Bid Kid Adieu," is a classic that every sports writer should read—but they are not the stuff of the daily sports pages. They

weren't written while fans stomped their feet and loudspeakers blasted music and the clock ticked down on the game and the deadline. They weren't written to fit a 20-inch news hole or to be subbed in a later edition.

The sports writing we will look at was done on the run yet has the wonderful, creative flair of polished pieces that have been labored over as if time didn't matter. They have phrases that make us smile in the morning, then linger in our minds all day like a tune we can't stop whistling. They are the game stories, columns, and features that really do sing.

Beat Reporting

Beat writers are the backbone of every sports staff. The best ones work the hardest, put in the most hours, and write the most stories. They know everything about their sport and are kind enough to help out hotshot columnists or feature writers who tread on their territory.

Beat writers show up for a baseball game 3½ hours before the first pitch and make the rounds of clubhouses, dugouts, and batting cages, talking to players, coaches, the manager, and, a good deal of the time, each other. They bat out their early notes, craft their gamers, go down to the locker rooms for more quotes, rewrite their stories, then hang around the silent ballpark working on more notes and sidebars long after the elevator operators go home.

They cruise empty basketball arenas during the day looking for a coach or general manager to get some inside dope. They watch shootarounds and work the locker rooms until the doors close. They go to early-morning workouts at the racetrack, foot-

Michelle Kwan of Lake Arrowhead, Calif., performs her routine on her way to the silver in the ladies final in the International Skating union's Grand Prix Final at Tokyo's Yoyogi Gym on Saturday, Feb. 17, 2001. (AP Photo/Katsumi Kasahara)

ball practices on rainy afternoons. They schmooze with agents and flacks and trainers. They scrawl everything they see and hear in their little notebooks or on yellow legal pads, a lot of stuff that will never get into print, a tidbit or two that will. Once in a while, they come up with a scoop that makes headlines.

Beat writers live to break news. A good writer who covers a team knows every trade, every move, and the dollar amount of every deal—before it happens. The beat writer keeps up with all the injuries and knows that a fractured metatarsus is a broken foot and probably means four to six weeks on the disabled list, whereas a torn ACL can end a season, if not a career. If a ballplayer is arrested, the beat writer knows the charges, the date of the arraignment, and the lawyer's phone number before the team or the city desk finds out.

Yet at the heart of every beat writer's life is the game, the race, the fight, the match, giving readers the details and quotes they didn't get on television or radio, validating what they did see or hear, and adding insight and perspective. At their best, beat writers tell a story so compellingly that readers love it whether or not they saw or listened to the game the day before. Over a long season, when one game might blur into another, a sharp beat writer finds those unique moments in each game that lift a story out of the ordinary.

Beat writers, at least as much as columnists, give a sports section its edge. They can be aggressive or easy or a little of both. They range around the history of their sport, assess the present, and set the tone for the future—all the time spinning stories of the people they cover. Players come and go; beat writers stay and talk to the next guys. Beat writers have to be people people, comfortable chatting with everyone and confronting anyone. Above all, good beat writers have to be knowledgeable, creative, accurate, professional journalists reporting the news the moment it happens.

A beat writer's life is defined by the season and the schedule, and his or her family has to adapt. A daughter who has a birthday on Memorial Day knows she will always have to settle for a long-distance kiss from her dad if he's the auto racing writer covering the Indy 500. Labor Day is

Overall leader Lance Armstrong of the U.S. rides past the Arc de Triomphe during the 20th and final stage of the Tour de France cycling race between Arpajon and Paris on Sunday, July 25, 1999. Armstrong rode to victory in the Tour de France on Sunday, capping an amazing comeback from cancer and becoming just the second American to win cycling's showcase race. (AP Photo/Laurent Rebours)

another day of work for tennis writers at the U.S. Open. Thanksgiving and Christmas dinners come late for football beat writers covering games those days.

Baseball writers have the toughest beat—the best or the worst, depending on the point of view and the kind of season their team is having. Major league baseball is 81 games on the road, 81 at home, plus spring training, playoffs, and the World Series. Baseball writers stand for nearly 200 versions of

Venus Williams hugs the Women's Singles trophy on Centre Court at Wimbledon, Saturday, July 8, 2000, after defeating defending champion Lindsay Davenport. Williams won the final 6-3, 7-6 (7-3). (AP Photo/Dave Caulkin)

the "Star-Spangled Banner," not all of which would be recognizable to Francis Scott Key. Some never stop typing, even through "the dawn's early light." And there is no off-season. They check out every whisper and wild rumor, every trade and signing all winter, and they can't wait until pitchers and catchers report for spring training to start over again.

Listen to *Boston Globe* columnist Bob Ryan, who pounded the basketball and baseball beats, covering the Celtics and Red Sox, at various times over the past 30 years:

> Anybody covering one of the four major beats [baseball, basketball, football, hockey] has the regular season when they actually play the games, and the rest of the year when they get ready to play the games. It's become this intense coverage, and most people, I guarantee, dread the off-season because it's a lot more aggravating. You don't even have the reward of the game. You have all the other stuff, and you get sick of getting bogged down in negotiations and chasing around agents. Then there are the drafts, which have taken on a life of their own. The preparation for the drafts is intense. It's all so encompassing.

Boxing writers know that fighters are the most colorful characters, and that trainers, managers, and promoters are the most wonderful liars and scoundrels—fine fodder for stories. The trick is to find out who is lying the most.

Golf writers wander from one posh course to another, staying in resorts, rental homes, or B&Bs near the course, trying to slip in a round or two a week. They work out of large white press tents, wear orange Velcro "media" armbands as they walk inside the ropes down the fairways, and kneel quietly on the edge of the green when Tiger Woods is putting. Sometimes they look at each other and wonder if life can get any better. Yet even that most pastoral of sports is tough to cover for a beat writer determined to do it right.

Each sport places its own demands on beat writers. The basics of good beat writing are the same—preparation, diligence, knowledge, passion, talent, competitiveness, among others—but how the writers go about it varies.

One of the best and most diligent in the business, Doug Ferguson of The Associated Press, has this to say about covering golf:

Imagine having a job outdoors, usually in perfect weather, the aroma of freshly cut grass and often a gentle sea breeze, walking storied courses such as Pebble Beach, Augusta National and the TPC at Sawgrass, an arm's length away from Tiger Woods, Ernie Els and Phil Mickelson. No wonder so many people think it's like stealing money.

What they overlook are the 14-hour days, a game that takes four days to determine a winner, and trying to keep tabs on over 200 players. And that's just the PGA Tour—golfers who are a team unto themselves, independent contractors who make their own schedules.

Clearly, there is more to covering golf than recording birdies and bogeys. Like any other sport, it involves identifying trends on the course and being aware of trouble off it, such as the suddenly cool relationship between Woods and his first caddie, Fluff Cowan, who eventually was canned. Beyond the game are issues such as equipment contracts (Tiger leaving Titleist for Nike), scheduling (top players skipping world-class events or taking appearance money to play overseas) and television contracts and coverage. Golf can be either the easiest gig around, or one of the most demanding. That depends on how much effort you choose to put into it.

Some beat writers will rarely, if ever, leave the press tent. They either watch on television (you might as well stay home), or simply wait for the leaders to tell them that they hit a 7-iron from 171 yards into 8 feet for a birdie on the 17th. They don't know what they're missing.

Exhibit A: Tiger Woods hit a 9-iron that came up just short on the 17th hole at Valderrama last year, and trickled back into the water. The next round on the same hole, his drive landed about 3 inches away from the divot he made the day before. He laughed about it with his caddie, decided to hit one club higher and landed it about 6 feet from the hole. The only way to know that is to be out there.

I try to walk at least nine holes a day, usually 18, and I think it's

Serena Williams, of Palm Beach Gardens, Fla., celebrates after defeating Lindsay Davenport, of Newport Beach, Calif., in the women's singles semifinals at the U.S. Open tennis tournament on Friday, Sept. 10, 1999, in New York. Williams won 6-4, 1-6, 6-4. (AP Photo/Kathy Willens)

imperative you see every hole at some point during the week. There are times I see nothing worth writing about. But I am certain of this—if I stay in the press tent, there's no way I would see anything. You have to give yourself a chance.

Granted, golf has the largest arena by far of the major sports. You see someone has made six straight birdies, and by the time you walk three miles to catch up with him, he's made two bogeys and is far down the leaderboard. It's impossible to be in the right spot all the time, but you have to try. If nothing else, you can get an idea of the conditions: whether approach shots are landing soft or bouncing high, whether a ball disappears in thick

Laila Ali of Miami Beach, Fla., right, connects against with Kristina King, of Muskegon, Mich., left, at Tian He stadium in the southern Chinese city of Guangzhou on Saturday, April 22, 2000. Ali won by technical knockout in the first major boxing event since the founding of the People's Republic of China. (AP Photo/Vincent Yu)

rough or sits up in rough that's not very deep.

One other example of why knowing the course is so critical. On Sunday at the LPGA Championship last year, I had seen Karrie Webb make a bogey on the 10th hole because she missed the green long and to the left. The pin was in the back left section, and it was impossible to chip close because of how the green sloped away from her. Later that afternoon, Juli Inkster was in a playoff with Stefania Croce when they got to the 10th. Croce missed it long and left. Her chip went 20 feet by the hole and she made bogey. Only having seen the course could I identify where the tournament was won or, in this case, lost.

Perhaps the best reason to get out on the course is this: The players see who walks the course and that translates into greater respect for you. That helps in the depth of answers you get in subsequent interviews.

But there is a tradeoff to spending a lot of time on the course. You can miss some contenders and big names as they finish their rounds. Some reporters will camp out on the 18th green and wait to talk to players as soon as they sign their cards. It's best to start the day by identifying players you need to talk to, being aware of when they finish and getting back to the 18th green in time.

And if there is a lull in the day, it's good to know the lightning rods. In Canada two years ago, I was reading a story from Europe about Colin Montgomerie, who has never won in America. About that time, Nick Faldo was finishing his round. I caught up with Faldo and asked him if he was surprised that Monty won't come over to America to face stiffer competition. Faldo was surprisingly blunt, saying Monty was comfortable collecting "fat checks" in Europe. Those comments served as the impetus of a feud between Faldo and Ryder Cup captain Mark James the next year.

Golf coverage these days goes beyond the players. I've always felt that most golf fans either want to play golf or buy a new driver. The equipment industry is important in that regard. Golf is unique in that writers and fans can play most of the same courses as the pros and use the same equipment. Key industry sources such as Wally Uihlein (Titleist) and Bob Wood (Nike) can keep you abreast of new products, and also offer insight into the players who use them. The late Ely Callaway was an excellent source when John Daly resumed drinking, for example, and when Arnold Palmer endorsed a driver that failed to meet U.S. Golf Association standards.

And while it's difficult to get to know so many players, they all have agents. A year ago, I "wasted" an entire day at the Byron Nelson Classic walking with the agents of young phenom Sergio Garcia, building a relationship that paid dividends the rest of the year. I also spent a round with Mark Steinberg, Tiger's agent, not seeing much golf but making a small deposit with the hope it would pay dividends. It did.

And that's really what beat coverage comes down to—relationships with the players, with industry sources, with PGA Tour management, with agents. And even a relationship with the golf course.

Ferguson and AP's longtime auto racing writer, Mike Harris, travel year-round covering their beats. Harris not only goes to every big race, he knows every driver, every mechanic, every sponsor. He knows where they ate dinner last night and where they'll probably eat tonight, and he just may join them for a bite and a chat. He visits drivers in their trailers and garages, calls their wives and children by their first names. Harris doesn't merely cover auto racing, he lives it.

Unlike beat writers at newspapers who focus on their local teams, most of the other AP beat writers are based at the Rockefeller Plaza headquarters in New York and cover their sports on a national or international level. They travel for special events and features and coordinate daily coverage from bureaus in every major city.

The three baseball writers in New York cover all the Yankees and Mets games, but also are responsible for overall coverage in the sport. They edit stories from ballparks day and night during the season, taking them on their computers from staff writers and stringers at each game and working them into nice, tight, right-to-the-point accounts. They count down the outs from the seventh inning on—"six outs to go . . . three to go . . ." and press the send button to shoot the stories onto the wire the moment the games end. Within seconds, the stories bounce back and forth between Earth and satellites and out to almost every newspaper in the United States.

The AP baseball beat writers go to spring training and selected games involving various teams around the country during the season. They write features, but more often stay with the news. When Cal Ripken Jr. ended his streak, AP baseball writer Ben Walker was there along with a staff suitable for the seventh game of the World Series. When Mark McGwire passed Roger Maris, Walker was there again, leading the pack. When owners and players met during the strike, Walker's baseball beat teammate, Ron Blum, waited outside the doors with his pen poised. Blum has the numbers

New Jersey Devils captain Scott Stevens kisses the Stanley Cup after the Devils beat the Dallas Stars 2-1 in double-overtime in Game 6 of the Stanley Cup finals in Dallas, Saturday, June 10, 2000. The Devils took the best-of-seven series 4-2. Stevens won the Conn Smythe trophy for the Stanley Cup playoffs most valuable player. (AP Photo/Donna McWilliam)

(phone, salary, probably Social Security, Visa, and American Express) on every player, agent, team owner, and official in baseball. No one dares not to call back Blum, not even, or perhaps especially, the commissioner. All beat writers should inspire at least a modicum of such respect and terror. Blum can carry on two, even three conversations at the same time, deftly juggling cell phones while he writes down notes, listens to a tape recording of an interview on the field a few minutes earlier, watches a rerun of a play on TV, keeps a box score, and types the story of a game in progress.

At the dozens of AP bureaus, sports writers are multifaceted beat writers for each of their teams, covering home games, practices, press conferences, drafts, and all the trades, injuries, and other news. The two San Francisco writers, for example, must be versatile and energetic enough to cover the 49ers, Raiders, Giants, Athletics, Sharks, college football and basketball at Stanford, California, and other colleges, plus golf tournaments, track and field meets, and other events. Every football game requires advance stories through-

out the week, a lead and often a sidebar for morning papers on game day, a separate story for afternoon papers, and follow-up stories for both cycles the next day. Every baseball, basketball, and hockey game requires morning and afternoon leads, notes, and, depending on the circumstances, sidebars.

Editors demand a lot of beat writers and count on them to deliver. There are no days off when there's a game or news about the beat. And good beat writers wouldn't want it any other way.

"Be first and don't get beat," *Los Angeles Times* sports editor Bill Dwyre tells his writers. "I hate getting beat. We're very competitive. We don't like the (Orange County) *Register* beating us. We don't like the (Los Angeles) *Daily News* beating us. We hate *The New York Times* to come in here and beat us.

"Beat people here have to work hard. Those are some of the toughest assignments around. Jason Reid covers the Dodgers for us and he wrote probably 450 stories last year."

New York Times sports editor Neil Amdur wants his beat writers to be as competitive and enterprising as he was when he covered tennis in the 1970s and 1980s. His predecessors and early colleagues, he recalls, were "the gentlemen from the *Times,*" who were regarded as "real nice and good and sweet."

"They were hard workers but no one ever associated them with grit and guts journalism," Amdur says. "I felt that aggressive reporting was one of my strengths. So when I became the editor here I vowed that I was going to hire people that were really tough and would be aggressive and that could dominate their beat in New York. That was my goal. I was not interested in sweetness and light."

Amdur recruited sharp, energetic beat writers over the past 10 years as he scrapped for readership among New York's sports fans.

"We're the only section on the paper here that has to take our ball and go to the tabloids' playground," he says. "Everybody else comes to the *Times*—for culture, for foreign, for national, for financial. They all come here to play and the *Times* kind of sets the table. But (in the sports section) we've got to take our ball

and go to the tabs' playground, take off our shirts and play on their court. We have to compete with them while still competing with the (Washington) *Post* and *USA Today* and *Sports Illustrated.* We try to look for ways and means that we can establish our identity while still preserving the integrity of the paper."

Editors at smaller papers are just as competitive.

"Part of our standards are never to get beat on a story," *Dayton Daily News* sports editor Dean Rock says. "But the reality is the (college) football coach can have a contract with the local TV station, and the TV station is going to place certain stories. So I don't know if it's fair of me to say never get beat on a story anymore. I can certainly still ask for critical, analytical copy, the insightful, clear and accurate copy. This paper needs enterprise, and I told our beat writers, 'Look, we're not going to just spew out the old standbys. You're going to have to write at least one story a month where you address some trend or issue. Throw the reader a bone. Give them something.' "

All sports writers, but particularly beat writers, have to be

With one skate in the crease, Dallas Stars right wing Brett Hull (22) shoots the Stanley Cup winning goal past the sprawling Buffalo Sabres goalie Dominik Hasek (39) in the third overtime period of Game 6 of the Stanley Cup Finals in Buffalo, N.Y., early Sunday morning, June 20, 1999. (AP Photo/Gene Puskar)

careful not to cross the border between being friendly with players, agents, owners, and other sources, and being friends with them.

"The hazard is that you don't write what you know because you don't want to offend anyone, you want them to like you," AP sports editor Terry Taylor says. "The most sickening sight in the world to me is to see a manager or a coach or front-office person go over to a beat writer and slap him on the back and treat him like a buddy. That tells me something's wrong with this picture.

"There's a professional relationship. Beat writers may write things that are unpleasant, but as long as they are truthful and fair, I think that's the mark of men and women doing their jobs. You're not put on a beat to be anybody's buddy. You're there to report. Sometimes that line gets crossed. There's far too much that the public has a right to know. We would be fairly worthless if we went in and wrote just love letters."

As a writer for the AP, which serves 1,500 U.S. newspapers and thousands more overseas, I long ago embraced a neutral stance on all sports and a detached, sometimes adversarial relationship with the people I covered. I jettisoned my teen-age love of the Knicks, Dodgers, and Jets and came to admire, if not feel any affection for, the dreaded Celtics, Yankees, and Giants. I rooted for the story, silently pulling for anything or anyone that would make the story livelier, stronger, better to write, and as soon as possible before deadline. At Wimbledon last year, I secretly wanted Pete Sampras to win and break the men's all-time Grand Slam title record with his parents watching him in the Centre Court stands for the first time. I thought that would be a better story than Patrick Rafter stopping Sampras, though Rafter could also be a compelling tale, coming back from a career-threatening shoulder injury. Two months later, I quietly rooted for Marat Safin, the charismatic young Russian, to beat Sampras in the final because that would be more historic and theatrical. Over the years, I came to thrive on the excitement of the event and the power of the performances, to get pumped up by the special quality and drama of the moment rather than the identity of the victor.

That doesn't mean a beat writer, especially one for a newspaper serving one city, cannot be a fan of the hometown team, passionately dishing out praise and scorn. It's a tricky issue, but some very good writers, like the *Boston Globe*'s Bob Ryan, pull it off without compromising their integrity.

"I've never made any secret of the fact that I feel I'm first and foremost a fan," Ryan says. "I go to games I don't have to, games I've paid for tickets. It's important that people can relate to you that way. Beyond that, I'm going to bring some sense of knowledge, which I think they accept. I think I can relate to what a fan is thinking. But covering a team, there are ways to write it. It helps you write if you can talk about it from a point of view. There are times you write stories about how this awful atrocity was perpetrated upon the team, and if you follow the team this is the way you would think. You try to phrase it so that it's not you who is personally outraged, but you know the fan is personally outraged.

"I wanted the team to win. First of all, I thought it was a lot better for everybody when the team won. It made your life easier. In Boston, you can't cover a team and not try to reflect the vibrations of the town. That would be ridiculous. It's not a clinical analysis thing; it's got to be a blood and guts thing. I never made any secret about writing it from a blood and guts viewpoint. But that doesn't eliminate criticism. It goes completely in concert. When things are going well, you write it from that kind of an emotional standpoint. When things are going poorly, it's still emotional; it's just that you're reflecting it's a negative emotion. I wouldn't be able to go about it any other way. Some beat guys maintain a scholarly detachment. That's not me. I'm not scholarly detached. I'm emotional and I love these games. I still love baseball and basketball very, very much."

All of Ryan's passion for basketball, all his deep knowledge of the history of the sport, and all his skills as a writer came into play in a game story he remembers in detail 15 years later and still savors as one of his best and most satisfying: the epic game between Boston and Chicago in the 1986 NBA playoffs when Michael Jordan scored 63 points in double overtime against the Celtics—and lost.

It was an afternoon game with no frantic deadline pressure. The writers had the time on this one to do their research, reflect on what happened, and tell the story with style. All the Boston and Chicago writers walked out of Boston Garden together to go out to eat at 10 o'clock—more than six hours after the game ended.

"I had gotten it, and in my mind then and now nobody on this earth has ever had a chance to do it better," Ryan said. "I was up for the big occasion. To me, people are going to look for that story in 50 years, and they're going to find everything they want to know about that game."

That's what all beat writers want to feel when they're walking out drained after pouring themselves into the story of a big event—the sense that they nailed it and that their words measured up to the Jordanesque performance they had just seen.

If the days of the "gentlemen from the *Times*" are gone, it is in part because journalism has changed over the years, just as everything else has changed.

Newspapers, radio and TV stations, and Internet sites are sending more and more staffers to games—especially playoff and championship games. In big media crowds, an invasion of thousands with giant credentials dangling from their necks during the Super Bowl and just a bit fewer for the World Series, Final Four, and NBA Playoffs, the beat writers have to jostle for elbow room with everyone else and never get any quiet moments with the people they cover in less obtrusive circumstances the rest of the year. Access is regimented and restricted, interview sessions are formal and stiff, and everyone is more guarded as they stare out at strangers and a sea of cameras and microphones. In general, it seems the larger the event and the more reporters who are crammed in, the harder it is to produce lively, outstanding stories.

"The Super Bowl is a huge bore for most regulars—the same stuff you've heard all year gets regurgitated in massive gang bangs," says AP football writer Dave Goldberg. "The way to get around that is to find a story that most other people aren't writing. It may not be at the venue: Call relatives, friends, old coaches and team-mates and you can often get a pretty good feature. Carlton Bailey was a relatively obscure Buffalo linebacker who was playing in the Super Bowl while the Gulf War was on. His father, an Army sergeant, was in the gulf. Hal Bock was doing the story and spent half the week trying to get a phone number for Mrs. Bailey, Carlton's mom. He finally tracked her down in Baltimore and her first words were, 'I hope that SOB gets his ass shot off.' Actually, it turned into a pretty good story.

"Much of the Super Bowl is non-news that gets hyped—a misquote by a New Orleans broadcaster (third hand) in which Jim McMahon allegedly called the women of New Orleans 'sluts'; McMahon mooning a helicopter; a drunken bar 'fight' between Darrell Talley of Buffalo and Magic Johnson's bodyguard. You should look for the offbeat. My favorite quote came from Marv Levy when he was asked if the Super Bowl was a 'must win' for the Bills: 'No. World War II was a must win.'

"There are also phony stories, particularly at the Super Bowl, like 1990, when a tabloid TV type reported the NFL had covered up positive drug tests for three famous quarterbacks, believed to be Joe Montana, Dan Marino and Jim Kelly. In 1986 everyone was checking out rumors that Montana's back surgery was really drug rehab. It was a huge tempest and Montana, who was playing in the game, was on the defensive the entire week. The Niners still won 55-10 and he was the MVP."

Goldberg is a beat writer who roams around the country during the season, covering games, stockpiling information, building contacts with players, coaches, and officials from many teams, but not overlooking other good sources. He is one of the great schmoozers in the business, a big, burly, friendly man who has a cutting wit and a discerning eye. Any football writer would be wise to pick up on his insights and methods:

Hard news often comes from assistant coaches, trainers (if the coach isn't paranoid, and many are), equipment managers, second-level front office people, even some PR people who will be fairly candid off the record in their assessments of teams, play-

Former Chicago Bulls' star Michael Jordan kisses the basketball floor of Chicago Stadium as he leaves it for the last time, Friday, September 9, 1994. Jordan played in a charity basketball game after completing his first season playing Double-A baseball for the Birmingham Barons. The stadium is due to be torn down and the Bulls will be playing at the new United Center across the street from the stadium. (AP Photo/Barry Jarvinen)

ers, etc. NFL PR people also are full of gossipy items about other teams. But approaches are different. National guys like me often get better access and more interesting stuff from GMs, even owners. Carmen Policy loves national guys, and old-line owners like Dan Rooney, Wellington Mara, Ralph Wilson and Lamar Hunt are often good sources. So are publicity-seeking newer owners, like Jerry Jones (although you can talk to him for an hour, then look at your notebook, and there's nothing there of substance).

One thing never changes: preparation, whether it's for the draft, a game, playoffs or the Super Bowl. Playoffs and the Super Bowl are usually easier, because in my case I've usually covered those teams a lot during the season. I go into the draft armed with as much info as I can—not only from the month or so before the draft, and not only from talking to personnel people and scouts (they lie and if they don't, they contradict each other). I do personal scouting—when I'm on the road I watch as much college football as I can and I have some idea of strengths and weaknesses, especially of skill players.

Perhaps no sport could be more different from football than figure skating. About all they seem to have in common is tremendous

New York Knicks' Buck Williams (52) fouls Indiana Pacers' Jalen Rose during second quarter action in the opening game of the second round of the NBA playoffs in Indianapolis, in this May 5, 1998, photo. (AP Photo/Michael Conroy)

popularity. The AP's Barry Wilner covers both, applying the same general principles and skills in different circumstances:

Among the things I've always done to prepare to cover skating:

• Get to know the skaters as well as possible. Unlike in team sports, they are far more personable in one-on-one conversations—they act like real people most of the time. Also cultivate a good relationship with their coaches, who often do the speaking (and thinking) for many skaters, and with the families, who have such a big stake in how the skaters perform.

• Nowadays, there also are publicists and agents who need to be stroked, at times, to get access to the skaters. But it isn't as bad as in other sports. Yet.

• Know the strengths and weaknesses of each skater. Is he or she a better jumper or artist? Does the skater do anything unique? What kind of music does the skater favor and what music best complements the skater's style and personality?

• At the U.S. championships, it is easier to have something in common to break the ice with new skaters. It could be something geo-graphical or about school or music or food, almost anything typically American.

• This is more difficult with foreigners at other competitions. While they are more trusting of the U.S. media now, it still isn't an open relationship. I am lucky to have a stringer who works with me, knows everyone and speaks eight languages. When I am on my own in those environments, I often have relied on other skaters or coaches I know well to help me break the ice or to give me good tidbits about the foreign skaters.

• You must be able to identify the jumps and the spins and the moves. Unless you are a skater, the best way to learn them is from a coach or a skater, and by carefully observing. It took me about three years before I was comfortable identifying them myself.

• You must understand the scoring system. It's really not that difficult, and a little research is all that is needed. If in doubt, ask a coach or a judge.

• Have a sense of humor about the sport. Unlike many other sports, it is so based in artistry (and absurdity) that it can be written with more of an offbeat touch. If Alexei Urmanov looks like a peacock in one of his outfits, say so.

What it all comes down to in any sport is hard work and long hours, a desire to be fast and first with the news and, perhaps most of all, a love of words and a love of the beat. Anything less is a recipe for burnout or mediocrity. Some writers cover a beat for an entire career and want nothing more. Others switch beats every few years and feel they grow with each one. Virtually every columnist and editor has cut his or her teeth in the business by covering beats. They are the essence of the sports pages and the place where sports writing careers begin. Michael Wilbon,

the *Washington Post* columnist and former college sports beat writer, puts it this way:

"Kids now want to be a columnist right away out of college. Nobody wants to do any reporting. It's ridiculous. Become a beat writer for 10 years first. Opinions ought to be grounded in something, like years and years of knowledge and working locker rooms and seeing games and having some perspective and something to refer to. It's still a news paper, or it ought to be. Without beat writers, there's no information. The columnist's job doesn't start until the beat writer reports the news. The beat writer breaks the story that sets everyone in motion."

Woods Closes Out U.S. Open Romp

By DOUG FERGUSON
AP Golf Writer

PEBBLE BEACH, Calif. (AP)—Tiger Woods' last challenge came from history. And like everything else for him at this U.S. Open, it was no contest.

Woods turned Pebble Beach into his personal playground, leaving everyone else so far behind that he might as well have been playing all alone. While the rest of the field was playing for second, Woods took aim at the record books.

When the final putt fell Sunday against the spectacular scenery off Carmel Bay, Woods claimed the U.S. Open, along with the kind of records no one imagined possible.

- He became the first player in the 106-year history of the U.S. Open to finish 72 holes at double digits under par—12 under.
- His 15-stroke victory not only shattered the Open mark of 11 set by Willie Smith in 1899, but was the largest ever in a major championship, surpassing the 13-stroke victory by Old Tom Morris in the 1862 British Open.
- His 272 tied the lowest score ever in a U.S. Open, first set by his idol, Jack Nicklaus, in 1980 and later matched by Lee Janzen in 1993.

"The day, and all week, I had a sense of calmness that I haven't had in quite a while," Woods said. "It was reminiscent of Augusta in '97. No matter what happened, I was able to keep my composure and focus on the shot I needed to make."

More history awaits next month. Woods goes to the British Open at St. Andrews with a chance to become only the fifth player—and at age 24, the youngest—to win all four major championships.

"He'll really have to be on his game to have a chance against us, won't he?" said Nick Faldo, rolling his eyes.

Too bad for Ernie Els and Miguel Angel Jimenez that the U.S. Open didn't have a B-flight this year. They had to settle for second place, at 3-over 287, their names in the record books, but only as footnotes.

This U.S. Open was really the Tiger Woods Classic.

"I don't know how much more there is to say," Els said. "We've been talking about him for two years. I guess we'll be talking about him for the next 20. When he's on, we don't have much of a chance.

"He's near perfect, the way he played this week."

So dominant was this performance that Woods never made worse than par over his final 26 holes. He closed with a 4-under 67, the best score of the day.

Jimenez had a 71, while Els finished with a 72. Woods began the final round with a 10-stroke lead, and no one got any closer than eight.

"Before we went out, I knew I had no chance," Els said.

Woods said his first U.S. Open victory was the perfect Father's Day present, even though Earl Woods did not make the trip to Pebble Beach.

"It was awesome, totally awesome," Earl Woods said from his home in Cypress. "It was like watching a Mercedes climb a hill. The power was there, the control was there. It's just on cruise control."

Even though the outcome was never in question, Woods managed to provide plenty of thrills on a lazy, sunny day along the rugged California coastline.

The gallery occupied every inch of grass along every fairway and behind every green, craning their necks to catch a glimpse of history. Yachts crammed into Stillwater Cove, and spectators tried to catch a piece of history from the beach below the famous "Cliffs of Doom" that overlook the Pacific.

They weren't watching a competition, but another coronation.

The first one came three years ago at Augusta National, where Woods became the youngest Masters champion with a record 12-stroke victory.

The U.S. Open was never supposed to look this easy. It is the toughest test in golf, which aims to identify the best player in the world.

Any questions?

Woods has now played in 14 majors as a professional and won three of them, including the PGA Championship in August. A sign dangling from the grandstand read, "Thanks, Jack. Long Live Tiger." Nicklaus

made his exit from a record 44th consecutive U.S. Open on Friday.

Woods is only just beginning.

It might have seemed as though he was playing in a different tournament than everyone else. Perhaps he simply is playing a different game.

Just as he had done from the start, Woods did everything required of a U.S. Open champion—and more. He hit fairways, often the middle stripe left by the lawn mowers, and hit more greens in regulation than anyone.

"Nobody else seems to be playing up to his level," said Tom Kite, who won the 1992 U.S. Open at Pebble Beach. "No one is scrambling the way he is. No one is pitching, chipping, putting the way he is. You need competition. Otherwise, it gets boring."

Mark O'Meara added: "If you were building the complete golfer, you'd build Tiger Woods."

It was the third major championship for Woods. Among active players, only Faldo (6) and Seve Ballesteros (5) have won more. Woods won the Pebble Beach National Pro-Am four months ago, and thus joined Ben Hogan (Riviera in 1948) and Nicklaus (Pebble in 1972) as the only players to claim a U.S. Open on the same course where they had won a regular tour event in the same year.

Woods pulled off a stunning comeback in February, making up seven strokes over his last seven holes with spectacular shots that have defined his career.

This time, he was brilliant over 72 holes and made a mockery of a U.S. Open that prides itself in protecting par.

It did just that—for everyone but Woods.

"For Tiger to break par the way he has shows how he has separated himself not just from present-day golfers, but from golfers from the past, as well," Phil Mickelson said.

Woods played the front nine with all pars. Then, as if sensing records were in range, poured it on with one spectacular shot after another.

He birdied four of the first five holes on the back nine, and saved par from a bunker on 17 with a shot that nearly went in.

"I played with him today, and it was just awesome to watch," Els said. "Anything I say is going to be an understatement."

After the final putt fell, Woods kissed the trophy and held it aloft. It was his 100th professional start, including unofficial events, and he won the 100th U.S. Open.

"That's what I had in mind," he said, as the crowd laughed at his blunt reply. "Well, I'm honest."

Woods' victory was his 20th on the PGA Tour, making him the only active player to achieve lifetime exemption—although he'll have to wait until 2010 to have put in the required 15 years.

Woods won for the 12th time in his last 21 tour events, and the 14th time in his last 25 tournaments worldwide, a staggering rate. He also improved to 18-2 in tournaments where he has had at least a share of the 54-hole lead.

Woods took the lead in the fog Thursday with a birdie from the bunker on the 18th hole. He never gave it back, becoming only the fifth wire-to-wire U.S. Open champion and first since Tony Jacklin in 1970.

It also was the first time Woods had led a tournament from start to finish.

The rest of the U.S. Open—that other tournament that was going on—had an international flavor.

John Huston had a 70 to finish fourth at 288, followed by European Ryder Cup teammates Lee Westwood and Padraig Harrington at 289. Faldo finished sixth, his best showing in a major since the '96 British Open. Vijay Singh tied for eighth, the best U.S. Open performance by a Masters champion in 10 years.

The Show Is Jordan's—But Celtics Steal It
Bulls Fall in 2 OTs, 135-131

By Bob Ryan, Globe Staff

Only one man in the history of the NBA playoffs knows what it feels like to score 63 points at the highest level of competition and be denied the sweet smell of team success. But the hoop world knows that every other player and every other team is on borrowed time. The Celtics, Lakers, Hawks, Rockets and every other 1986 title aspirant had better seize whatever opportunity they can—Now!—because we are clearly at the dawn of the Age of Jordan.

"I would never have called him the greatest player I'd ever seen if I didn't mean it," said Larry Bird after yesterday's exhilarating, stimulating, emotional, exhausting and altogether brilliant contest. "It's just God disguised as Michael Jordan."

Bird's equation of Jordan to the Deity is understandable in light of Jordan's record-breaking 63-point effort in the Garden (a display that surpassed Elgin Baylor's 1962 play-off standard of 61), but let the record show that Bird was able to speak in the pleasant afterglow of victory. Despite all Jordan's virtuosity, the Celtics constructed a 2-0 series lead by walking (staggering would be a more apt description) off with a 135-131 double-overtime triumph in what could accurately be described as an epic contest.

They play 'em and we rate 'em, and there is no question that this game will make the Top 5, and maybe even the Top 3, of Greatest Celtic Play-off Games Ever among the Garden cognoscenti. This was pure athletic theater, and not until Orlando Woolridge air-balled a desperation three-pointer with two seconds remaining in the second OT was there a legitimate chance for any Celtic owner, general manager, coach, player or fan to relax and light up that mental cigar. As long as Mr. Jordan is known to be present in this hemisphere, no rival lead is safe, no palm is dry, no throat swallows easily and no stomach is settled. A man who scores 63 points out of the flow is a man to fear, respect and idolize.

But justice, as we witnessed in Holmes-Spinks II, has nothing to do with winning and losing, for despite Jordan's 22 field goals and 63 points, he didn't make the biggest basket of the long, long afternoon. Jerry Sichting, a player whose game is to Jordan's as a 1955 Studebaker is to a 1986 Porsche, had that honor. For it was Sichting who took an inside-out pass from Kevin McHale and did what he has done faithfully all year—swished the foul line jumper. That basket broke the game's 13th tie and gave the Celtics a 133-131 lead with 57 seconds left in the second OT. And when Jordan missed a left baseline jumper on the next Chicago possession, Robert Parish rebounded.

The ball went to Bird (36 points, 12 rebounds, 8 assists), who orchestrated a two-man game on the right wing with Parish. "As soon as he set the pick and rolled, I gave it to him," said Bird, unconcerned that Parish had not scored a jumper all night and had established a bad case of the oopsies in his infrequent drives to the hoop. "When he goes, you've got to give him the ball. You don't worry about Robert Parish. I never do, because he's made a lot of big plays for this team."

That's no lie, and this time he took the pass and swished a 12-foot moon shot on the right baseline to give Boston a four-point lead (135-131) with nine seconds remaining.

The best shot Chicago could get was the weak Woolridge three-pointer. The ball was inbounded to Bird, who just stood with it to await the ending of a truly spectacular afternoon of play-off basketball.

In any game such as this, there is invariably an individual of whom it can safely be said, "Without him, this would definitely have been an L." Yesterday afternoon, that man was the oft-maligned Danny Ainge.

You never would have pegged Ainge as a potential hero midway through the third quarter. He hadn't even scored a point by the time the aggressive young Bulls claimed their final 10-point lead (69-59). But before the period was over, he had erupted for 13, including 11 in the final 2:36, the last three of which came on a three-pointer that brought the struggling Celtics within one at 84-83.

Ainge would wind up with 24, and he would score two giant baskets, the first a left-handed lane drive that would tie the score at 125-125 with 12 seconds left in the first OT, and the second an open 18-footer that would give Boston a brief 131-127 lead in the second OT, a lead that was quickly wiped out via two quick hoops by the irrepressible Jordan.

Chicago abandoned the first-game strategy of continual Jordan isolations, and he proved how brilliant he was by performing even better in the context of a normal offense than he did when 90 percent of the action was directed his way. The Bulls took the lead at 4-2 and clung to it stubbornly until a clock-beating 28-foot three-pointer by Bird gave Boston the lead at 93-92 and created the first of nine consecutive lead changes through 102-100, Boston (an inside-out three-pointer by Bird from McHale).

Boston did everything but summon the ghost of Walter Brown in an attempt to knock out the Bulls, but the visitors would not succumb. A 108-104 fourth-quarter lead soon turned into a 111-110 Chicago advantage on the Jordan basket that gave him an even 50 points. A 116-113 lead with 45 seconds remaining in regulation (an Ainge-to-McHale alley-oop) evaporated when Charles Oakley hit a free throw with 34 seconds left, leading to the sequence (Bird miss, Parish momentary rebound and Chicago steal/strip/maul/who-knows-what-but-no-call) that set up the game's most controversial happening.

Leading, 116-114, with six seconds left, the Celtics had to dig in one last time to preserve the lead. With about one second left, Jordan up-faked Dennis Johnson and threw up a three-pointer that clanged off the rim as McHale arrived on the scene.

Referee Ed Middleton called a foul on McHale after the shot. Did Jordan get hit? Did he spread-eagle smartly upon release and hit McHale? Do you ever make a call like this? Middleton did, and Jordan, naturally, sank both shots to create OT No. 1.

The Bulls surged ahead by four (123-119) on a Jordan three-point play with 1:39 left, but Sichting canned a corner jumper (missing the affixed free throw) and Ainge came through with that clutch drive. Jordan missed an unmolested left-side jumper and Bird rebounded with two seconds left. A Bird three-pointer was long and the weary troops entered the second OT.

Way, way back in this one, many amazing things had gone on. For example, Bill Walton (who fouled out with 6:10 left in regulation) grabbed 13 rebounds in 13 first-half minutes. Sidney Green and Oakley had made breathtaking tap-ins. Bird, after going 0 for 5 in the first quarter and then hyperextending his right pinkie (forcing him to play with it taped to its neighbor), came out to hit nine of his next 11 shots, including two three-pointers. McHale scored a fourth-quarter basket while actually sitting on Dave Corzine. And every primary Celtic had gotten himself into foul trouble (the first six guys, Walton being No. 6, compiled 31 fouls).

All the while, Jordan just kept scoring. And scoring. And scoring. This way. That way. Horizontally. Vertically. Diagonally. In ways never conceived of by Hank Luisetti, Joe Fulks, Paul Arizin or even World B. Free. And, reminded Parish, "It's not like he was doing it in a summer league."

A question now arises: What is Michael Jordan capable of doing in his own building? Two-and-zero looks about 100 times better than 1-1 right now.

It's Up, It's Good
Houston Sends Knicks to Round 2

By SELENA ROBERTS
New York Times

MIAMI—There was the deafening noise, and still Alonzo Mourning's baritone voice was able to cut through a vibrating Miami Arena as he cried out: "One stop. One stop." One surreal instant later, Allan Houston put down a forceful dribble, curled around Dan Majerle as tightly as a stripe on a candy cane and discovered a shaft of light.

With a clear view of the basket, Houston planted a foot on the free-throw line, tilted forward and tossed destiny up in the air. As his 10-foot jumper licked the front of the rim, bounced up and hung as if filled with helium, there dangled Jeff Van Gundy's job as the Knicks' head coach, Patrick Ewing's future and the path of the franchise.

Then, gravity brought down the Heat and devastated Coach Pat Riley as Houston's shot touched the backboard and fell softly into the net with just eight-tenths of a second left. The lead, Game 5, and another dramatic series with their loathed rival belonged to the Knicks in an unfathomable 78-77 victory that eliminated the Heat for the second time in three years. The Knicks advanced to the second round of the playoffs and will play the Hawks in a four-of-seven-game series to begin Tuesday in Atlanta.

"It's not about me," Van Gundy said. "I didn't do anything today. I just rode these guys. It says a lot about the character of this team that they stuck with me. I'm thankful for that."

Somehow, it seemed fitting that it was one of Van Gundy's core supporters, Houston, who shrugged off his flat start to this game and delivered the game-winning shot that propped up a Knicks team teetering on extinction.

"You can only put so much into a shot," said Houston, who made just 1 of his first 7 shots in the game but was 2 for 3 in the fourth period. "If we didn't get the bounce, we'd be talking about something totally different right now."

Instead, the floor was open for a discussion about a Knick team that would not die, about a former outcast finding his niche among the tenacious, and about an aging center standing up to his Georgetown apprentice, Mourning, and beating pain.

"Mr. Breaks Down," Van Gundy said with a smile, referring to Ewing. "Amazing, but he came through again."

It was Latrell Sprewell and Ewing who allowed Houston to be in the position to win the game. After the Heat took a 3-point lead with 58.5 seconds left, Ewing fought off Mourning, grabbed an offensive rebound and was fouled hard. With his right side aching from a third-quarter rib injury, with his Achilles' tendon throbbing through the tape, Ewing coolly hit two free throws to pull the Knicks within a point, 77-76, with 39.7 seconds left.

Then Tim Hardaway, the bane of the Knicks during three straight playoff meetings, dribbled the ball up the court and was beginning to drive past Charlie Ward when Sprewell cleverly stuck his hand in and poked the ball from him with 24.9 seconds left.

"It feels bad," Hardaway said. "I didn't come through, especially at that moment."

Then a snapshot of the defensive intensity of this game unfolded. Terry Porter harassed Sprewell, bumping and banging him with his forearm and body. Sprewell tried to free himself for a shot, but Porter forced him toward the sideline. Sprewell lost the ball, but the official ruled it went off Porter with 4.5 seconds left. That was the prelude to the inbound pass to Houston and the shot.

"It seemed like it hung for 2 minutes, not 2 seconds," Houston said. "It's the biggest shot ever for me."

It carried so much weight. It meant the Knicks became only the second No. 8–seeded team to beat a No. 1–seeded team. It left Riley heartsick after another first-round exit at the hands of his former team. It meant everything to Van Gundy's job stability. "After the game, I just went in and told him, 'Thanks for staying with it,' " Van Gundy said of Houston. "He did. He'd been struggling. But he needed to be in there."

Next to him were Ewing, Sprewell, Ward and Larry Johnson. Ewing led the team with 22 points and 11 rebounds, Sprewell added 14 points off the bench and Johnson came up with 13 points. They were the ones entrusted with the outcome of the game. But as wrenching as the finish was, the Knicks may have won this game in the first quarter.

They were down, 21-8, and on the verge of being knocked out of this series-deciding game early, just as they had been in Game 7 two years ago. That was a game in which Houston started out 1 for 9, a game the Heat owned from the start. This time, Chris Childs, limping off the bench with a thigh bruise, pushed the ball, looked for Sprewell running down the floor and took the Knicks on a 13-0 run to tie the score.

"I don't know about what has happened in the past," Sprewell said. "But this time, we wanted it. We wanted it with everything we had. When you're out there, you can't believe you're part of a game like this. It was draining emotionally, physically, everything. I've never been in a situation like this."

He had never seen one shot unleash so much pandemonium. As Houston's jumper was swallowed by the net, Ewing let out a howl and Sprewell ran in circles around the court with an elated Johnson.

"I was just hoping one of Charlie Ward's prayers would come true when that shot went up," Childs said, referring to his devout teammate. "I hoped that would help it go in."

One moment later, after Porter's desperation shot bounded off the rim at the buzzer, Houston stood on the court as he was hugged by his teammates and embraced by destiny. "It just feels good, well beyond that," Houston said. "It's all just so indescribable."

REBOUNDS: PATRICK EWING went up for a rebound in the third quarter and felt a pain in the lower right side of his rib cage. He was expected to have X-rays late Sunday night.... The Knicks will make a quick stop home and then travel to Atlanta on Monday, with the series to begin on Tuesday.... Miami is 14-24 in the playoffs and 8-9 against the Knicks.... The Knicks had no turnovers in the third quarter.... The Heat was led by ALONZO MOURNING's 21 points.... With CHRIS CHILDS on the floor in the first half, the Knicks were plus 18. They were minus 22 without him.

Assignments

1. Go to a game and write a 750-word story in a notebook or on a laptop computer within one hour of the end. Compare that story with those you see in the local and visiting team's paper or on the Internet the next day.

2. Quickly do research on the coach of one of your school teams or local pro teams using a team guide or information available online. Within two hours, write a 750-word story as if he or she had just retired.

3. Write a critique of two or three game or beat stories in the local papers, comparing how each used the same details. Which story did you like the best and why?

In the Trenches

Sports writers work amid chaos. They file from courtside as 20,000 fans roar and the press table rumbles and the band blasts "On Wisconsin" at deafening decibels a few feet away. They squeeze into cramped, humid locker rooms for quotes, race from one event to another, and fight deadlines every step of the way. They have to block out the noise, the pressure, the flashing lights. Or, perhaps more accurately, take it all in and filter out what they don't need.

In the sports department, there's a crisis every day, or at least the sports version of one. A four-team trade involving two future Hall of Famers. A famous head coach getting fired. A famous ballplayer getting arrested on drug charges or rape or murder, maybe all three. These are the stories that are going to make every paper the next day, that will have to be followed up for a couple of cycles, maybe a couple of days or weeks.

AP sports writers are used to chaos and never panic. In fact,

Los Angeles Lakers' Kobe Bryant (8) goes to the basket over Indiana Pacers' Dale Davis, lower left, and Austin Croshere (44) during the second quarter in Game 6 of the NBA Finals in Los Angeles, Monday, June 19, 2000. (AP Photo/Reed Saxon)

that is often when they shine brightest. From New York headquarters to bureaus in cities all over the country, writers and editors work together on crisis coverage as smoothly as basketball players running a weave up the court. For a journalist, it's a beautiful thing to behold.

Reporters in the field and in offices gather the facts, make the calls, go where they have to go, and get the story out. Speed is critical, accuracy essential. Bulletin, urgent, urgent add, 1st Lead-Writethru, 2nd Lead-Writethru, up to maybe a 26th Lead-Writethru, as in the case of the bombing at the Atlanta Olympics. They update and refine, clarify and correct, if necessary, until the whole thing is whittled down to a solid main lead and as many sidebars as the story deserves, all accompanied by boxes, lists, graphics, and photos.

Hours pass in what seems like minutes until finally it's done for the moment, or at least for this cycle, and everyone realizes they haven't eaten since breakfast, haven't even taken a bathroom break since sitting down. Exhaustion and relief mingle with a touch of pride. The story is out, already on the radio and television and Internet, and it will soon be in newspapers everywhere. It's time to relax, for a few minutes anyway, until the next crisis.

In the cracks of time between those adrenaline-rush stories and all the scheduled games that AP bureau sports writers handle, there is plenty of drudgery: reading and mostly discarding the press releases that arrive daily by mail and e-mail; culling the newspapers for clips to keep up the files; managing stringer coverage; organizing the paperwork that was supposed to disappear with the paperless society.

AP bureau sports writers do it all, the good, the bad, and the back-to-back night-day games. They are the utility players of sports writing, covering a broader range of major sports on a daily basis than anyone in the business.

Located in virtually every major city and some smaller ones, they are beat writers for all their teams, feature writers, state columnists, assignment editors, general reporters about everything in their territory. If it's a big news day—an election, an earthquake, a train wreck—they also

Michigan State's Mateen Cleaves, center, is embraced by his mother Frances, left, as his father Hank looks on after Michigan State won the NCAA Championship, Monday, April 3, 2000, at the RCA Dome in Indianapolis. Michigan defeated Florida 89-76. (AP Photo/Michael Conroy)

will work on that. They go to spring training and football camp, playoffs and championships, if their teams get that far. They don't travel with their teams during the regular season, but they have to keep track of every game. They cover the colleges and pros, and some cover high schools, too. Many bureau sports writers also are selected to cover events at the Summer and Winter Olympics as AP pulls together dozens of its best writers and editors from around the world to create the largest news contingent at the games.

The best bureau sports writers—Paul Newberry in Atlanta, Steve Wine in Miami, Joe Kay in Cincinnati, Alan Robinson in Pittsburgh, Nancy Armour in Chicago, Bob Baum in Phoenix, to name just a few—not only cover everything, they write with style and at no sacrifice of speed or accuracy.

On Martin Luther King Jr. Day this year, AP San Francisco sports writer Greg Beacham worked 16

Indiana head coach Bobby Knight screams at his players during the waning minutes of their team's 77-57 loss to Pepperdine in the first round of the East Regionals of the NCAA Tournament on Friday, March 17, 2000, at the HSBC Arena in Buffalo, N.Y. (AP Photo/Elise Amendola)

hours, covered three sports and wrote 3,000 words.

"Busy but not atypical," Beacham says.

This is how his day went:

- In the morning, he wrote a story from home on the San Francisco 49ers after making several calls regarding the departure of the offensive coordinator to become the Detroit Lions' head coach.

- In the afternoon, he covered a Golden State Warriors–Cleveland Cavaliers day game in Oakland, writing the game story, notes, and a follow-up lead.

- In the evening, he inched through rush-hour traffic to San Jose, 60 miles away, to cover a San Jose Sharks–Detroit Red Wings game, arriving 5 seconds before the puck dropped. He wrote the game story, notes, and a follow.

- When he arrived home just after midnight, he wrote another follow story on the Sharks–Red Wings, mostly for East Coast or Midwest papers that may have closed before the game ended.

That, Beacham says, wasn't even close to his busiest day, which came the previous year when he was the AP's Milwaukee sports writer. On that occasion he had bylines on the national sports wire from Green Bay, Madison, and Milwaukee, and he filed 5,400 words on the Packers, a University of Wisconsin football game, the Bucks, and a feature on Glenn Robinson.

As he talks about it now, Beacham is sitting at home at 5 P.M., eating a bowl of cereal while watching a hockey game. It's a relatively slow Friday. All he has done so far is file a nice, tight, well-written feature that will serve as an advancer for the U.S.-China soccer game he will cover the next day. In a few minutes, though, Beacham will go over to Oakland for a Warriors-Sonics game.

Newberry's byline appears on more than 500 stories a year, some big, some routine. "You have to know a little bit of everything, because you're going to get a little bit of everything," he says. "Probably the biggest thing, working for the AP in a job like this, is learning to manage time. You have to quickly figure out what's important, what's not. It helps to get some pretty good stringers you can rely on. You can't be in four places at one time, but sometimes it's almost like you've got to be. You have to be able to switch quickly from being at a basketball game one night to a hockey game the next night and a football game the next day. You've got to like a lot of different things and enjoy going from one to the other or it will quickly become a grind. That sort of fits with my personality. I don't think I'd like to cover one thing all the time, like a beat job with a newspaper. I wouldn't want to do baseball for eight months and then spend the off-season still following baseball. When a season ends, I like moving on and doing other stuff."

Here is the way Newberry spent one dizzying day last year:

It had been a long night.

I was looking forward to a nice, relaxing day at home after working into the wee hours at the 2000 Super Bowl. Sure, there was a hockey game between the Atlanta Thrashers and Pittsburgh Penguins, but that wasn't until 7:30 P.M. I would have plenty of time to take care of a few errands,

or just take it easy after a long, draining week and the thrilling championship game between the Rams and Titans.

Not so fast.

I heard a story on the radio shortly after I awoke: Two men had been stabbed to death in the trendy Buckhead nightclub district, apparently after an early-morning Super Bowl party. Then a call came from the office: There were rumors that an NFL player may have been involved.

It was going to be another long day for me and everyone in the AP's Atlanta bureau. I just didn't realize how long.

I volunteered to drive to Buckhead, about 40 minutes from my home, to look for witnesses and check out the nightclub where we thought the killings had occurred. It was closed. Most of the clubs in the area were shut down, too, and the sidewalks and shops were largely empty after a raucous week of revelry. In the meantime, my news editor had heard the NFL player was someone named Lewis from the Baltimore Ravens, so we began working the phones.

A spokesman for Jermaine Lewis said he wasn't even in Atlanta. I got in touch with Ray

U.S. Ryder Cup player Justin Leonard celebrates after sinking his putt on the 17th hole of his final round match, Sunday, Sept. 26, 1999 in Brookline, Mass. Leonard won the hole, clinching the Ryder Cup for the U.S. (AP Photo/Doug Mills)

Lewis' attorney, who said his client knew nothing about the killings but wouldn't say anything else. We suspected Ray Lewis was the man police were looking for.

I headed to the police station, where several reporters were already staked out, hoping to find out if anyone had been arrested and what Lewis' alleged role in the killing might have been.

The police weren't talking, but my office was. They called with another bit of big news: Baseball was suspending Braves pitcher John Rocker for his derogatory comments against gays, minorities, immigrants and just about anyone else in the human race.

The Braves were holding a news conference at 6:30 P.M., so another staffer from the bureau

AP newswoman Elisabeth Davis (right) interviews Tennessee reserve center Shalon Pillow of the Lady Vols, in Knoxville, Tenn. (AP Photo by Wade A. Payne)

replaced me at the police station and I headed to Philips Arena. That way, I could handle the news conference and also cover the hockey game, which was at the same building.

This is where things get a little confusing. In other words, just another wild day in the world of sports.

Ron Blum in New York was handling the main story on Rocker, so I fed him quotes from Braves president Stan Kasten and general manager John Schuerholz. I also called several Braves players at home and put together a 700-word reaction story to Rocker's suspension.

I had been watching the hockey game out of the corner of my eye on a television in the press room. When I saw the game was heading to the third period, it was time to start paying attention. Of course, the game went to overtime. I filed a 400-word lead, gathered quotes in the locker room and filed a 600-word optional story. Before I left the arena, I rewrote the stories on the hockey game and Rocker's suspension—another 1,300 words—for afternoon newspapers.

Oh, by the way, did I mention that sometime around 10 o'clock,

the Atlanta bureau learned that Ray Lewis was going to be charged with murder? They had that story on the wire within a few minutes, and I helped gather reaction from Ravens officials. I'm not sure when this happened, probably sometime around the time Jaromir Jagr scored a goal that sent the hockey game to overtime.

I was assigned to handle the PMs story on Lewis' arrest, so I headed back to Buckhead to see if anyone—bartenders, regular customers—had witnessed the previous night's events. One waitress had heard some commotion in the street, but she was too far away to see what happened. A few people grumbled to me about the growing crime problem in the area, which included a couple of other well-publicized slayings.

At about 3 A.M. Tuesday, I headed home to file my Lewis story. I finished up around 5 o'clock, beating sunrise but mumbling to myself that I had actually gotten to bed earlier after the Super Bowl.

As I drifted off to sleep, I thought about having to write a Rocker follow-up, more on Lewis' arrest, and whatever else came along tomorrow. Uh, make that today.

AP bureau sports writers often work from their homes or the ballparks and enjoy a certain freedom that other staffers might envy. But wherever they work, they have plenty to do. Those who do it well have tremendous energy, dedication, focus, and talent. To make it all fun and worthwhile, they also must have a love of sports and journalism. Some bureau sports writers enjoy it so much they choose to stay where they are for many years. Denne Freeman of Dallas and Harry Atkins of Detroit each worked as bureau sports writers for decades before retiring recently, and they were deeply respected among their peers locally and nationally. Others have chosen to work as bureau sports writers as a step toward jobs at newspapers or national writing positions with the AP in New York. An editor looking for someone with versatility, talent, and experience couldn't ask for anyone better than a bright writer with a few years working in an AP bureau.

Here's what Steve Wine of Miami has to say about it:

I can't imagine a better place for a young journalist to work and learn than an AP bureau. During my 13 years in Miami I've covered presidential campaigns and other natural disasters, crime and stockholders meetings, trials and funerals—and that's as a sports writer.

With a couple dozen AP reporters trying to cover the entire state of Florida, it's imperative that they be able to handle stories outside their areas of expertise. During one busy news week I found myself covering the United Mine Workers national convention. Such assignments are great experience, broaden your perspective and can only improve your skills.

Because of Florida's rapid growth, my job has evolved a great deal. When I came to Miami in 1987, there was one professional team in town and two in the state. Now there are four in South Florida and nine in the state. We have full-time sports writers in Miami, Tampa and Jacksonville, and reporters who split their time between news and sports in Miami and Orlando.

I'm responsible for coverage in South Florida, and my primary

Tiger Woods of the United States tries to coax a putt into the hole on the 12th green on the final day of the British Open Golf championship on the Old Course at St. Andrews, Scotland on Sunday, July 23, 2000. (AP Photo/Adam Butler)

Ferrari driver Michael Schumacher of Germany is cheered by his pit crew as he heads for the finish line to win the Australian Formula One Grand Prix in Melbourne, Sunday, March 12, 2000. Schumacher finished ahead of Ferrari teammate Rubens Barrichello, with Schumacher's younger brother, Ralf Schumacher, finishing third in the first grand prix of the season. (AP Photo/Rick Rycroft)

beats are the Miami Dolphins, Florida Marlins and Miami Heat. I don't travel with the teams, other than to some postseason games. Our other Miami sports writer handles the Miami Hurricanes and Florida Panthers, and we divvy up tennis, golf, horse racing, auto racing, boxing and the rest.

I often find myself at Dolphins camp writing about the Marlins, or at the Heat arena writing about the Dolphins. It's not unusual to have stories about two or three sports on the national wire in the same day. It's challenging trying to compete with beat writers for the local papers when you're spread so thin, but that makes scoops even more rewarding.

Sometimes the job is like being the sports editor at a medium-size paper, because there's a lot of administrative work involved. We rely heavily on stringers. I give them assignments, arrange for their credentials and make sure they get paid.

Freelancers make it possible for us to cover every game in the NBA, NHL and major league baseball, and they often help us get the jump on stories about trades, injuries and arrests. We once sent a stringer to an NHL owners meeting, and because it was expected to be routine, he was the only South Florida reporter there. He phoned me midway through the meeting and said, "You're not going to believe this, but Miami was just awarded an expansion franchise." We fell into that scoop just by showing up.

Nearly a year after Dolphins coach Jimmy Johnson retired, I wrote him a letter requesting an interview. He had been reclusive and inaccessible to the media since leaving the NFL, so I wasn't optimistic about a response. But a couple of weeks later, in the midst of the presidential election recount, I was in the bureau during a particularly frantic afternoon when Johnson called wanting to talk. I had a Bush-Gore story on my screen

and Jimmy Johnson on the phone: At the AP, that's considered a good day.

Sometimes the most engaging stories are found serendipitously away from the games that bureau sports writers cover routinely. Harry Atkins served as AP sports writer in Michigan for 29 years, covering the famous and the infamous, from Mark "The Bird" Fidrych and Sparky Anderson to Michigan's Fab Five, from Isiah Thomas and Barry Sanders to Dennis Rodman.

"I covered Dennis Rodman before he was a cross-dresser," Atkins says.

Yet some of his most memorable stories were offbeat but upbeat pieces that had little to do with winning or losing. Atkins was a master at finding those hidden gems and writing about them. In part, that was because he had talent and curiosity. Perhaps more important, he loved what he did.

As former Detroit news editor Paula Froke said in a tribute to Atkins upon his retirement, "That kind of spirit comes through time and again in Harry's writing. He writes stories . . . that are rich with detail and texture, stories that reach below the surface for meaning. He writes about the little guys as well as the big guys, the obscure as well as the obvious. He reports thoroughly, observes keenly, describes vividly. And he pulls it all together in a graceful, evocative and highly readable style."

That's the kind of writing that distinguishes the best sports writers—and the kind that is expected of AP bureau sports writers, no matter how heavy the load. Here is what Atkins says he searched for and found as he roamed Michigan.

They are stories that remind us that those are ordinary folks playing the games. Some stories can be found while covering a major beat, simply by looking around the corner. Or, in the case of Rip Collins, just by looking down the hall.

Collins was in charge of the visitors' clubhouse at old Tiger Stadium. He had parlayed a never-ending line of dirty underwear, crabby ballplayers and picking up after grown men into a comfortable living.

In his younger days, however, it turns out that Collins was a

Marine fighter pilot during the Korean War. He made 120 carrier landings during daylight and 50 more at night.

Sometimes you have to look for these stories. Once in a while, they just fall in your lap. The key for the writer is to realize there is a story waiting to be told, if handled with the right touch.

In 1992, on the agate page of the *Detroit Free Press,* I saw a brief note about Centreville High School pulling the plug on its football season with five games remaining. That struck me as odd. School officials were reluctant to discuss it on the phone. So, a few days later, I got in the car and made the three-hour drive.

It proved to be worth every minute.

The games were canceled because the team was hit hard with injuries and the coach felt there simply weren't enough healthy bodies left to field a team. Only 18 of the school's 283 students tried out for the varsity, and the coach felt his JV players were too small and inexperienced. He didn't want anyone else getting hurt.

Centreville, a charming town in the southwest corner of the state,

Ken Schrader (36) slams into Dale Earnhardt (3) during the Daytona 500 on Sunday afternoon, Feb. 18, 2001, at the Daytona International Speedway in Daytona Beach, Fla. Earnhardt was killed in the crash. Earnhardt, the driver people either loved or hated—but had to watch either way—died on Feb. 18, 2001, at the Daytona 500 from injuries sustained in this crash. (AP Photo/Glenn Smith)

was split by the move. Since the team continued to practice, some of the fathers felt their sons might as well be playing the games, too.

My day in Centreville produced a rare double-dip. The story was a budget item on both the national sports wire and the general news wire.

A sense of humor doesn't hurt, either.

In 1993, the Northern Michigan golf team couldn't practice because spring storms kept the Upper Peninsula blanketed with snow. The only time they got to tee it up was when they piled into the team van and drove five to eight hours to the Lower Peninsula for matches.

I caught up with the players at their league meet in Coldwater. They turned out to be a great bunch. Funny, self-effacing and full of laughs. And good quotes. It was a nice story.

In 1998, there was a 5-foot-5 guard named Earl Boykins play-

In the Trenches

NASCAR driver Jeff Gordon, from Pittsboro, Ind., jumps completely in the air from the roof of his DuPont Chevrolet after winning the Winston Cup Championship at the Atlanta Motor Speedway in Hampton, Ga., Sunday, Nov. 16, 1997. (AP Photo/John Bazemore)

ing basketball for Eastern Michigan. Boykins, known to his teammates as "Earl the Squirrel," could play. While researching a feature on Boykins, I decided to call his father, a policeman in Cleveland.

Good move.

Dad, as it turned out, was a basketball junkie himself. And he had a sense of humor. He recalled carrying young Earl around in a gym bag, keeping the youngster warm while the father played in pickup games around Cleveland. He also recalled telling Earl to sit on the edge of the couch while college recruiters were in the house—so his feet wouldn't be so high off the floor.

If you like writing these offbeat stories, let people know. Spread the word, much like a salesman prospecting for new customers.

That's how I learned of Val Keeney, a freshman softball pitcher at Kalamazoo College who wore a hockey helmet. Keeney's jaw had been shattered by a line drive during the third game of the season and had to be wired shut. Without the helmet, her season would have been over.

Kalamazoo's sports information director called me one day and said, "I think this might be your kind of story." He was right. I drove out a day later and watched her pitch at Alma.

About a month before the 1996 U.S. Open at Oakland Hills, I was having lunch in northern Michigan with Andy Sneddon, a writer for the *Petoskey News-Review.* "Would you like to do Ben Hogan's caddy?" he asked. "He's an old friend of my father."

That's how I got the delightful story of Dave Press, a husky kid who hitchhiked the 20 miles to Bloomfield Hills every day in 1951, lied about his age, and ended up toting the champion's bag in one of history's most memorable Opens.

And, finally, don't be afraid to try something special with something ordinary.

In 1995, while covering spring training in Lakeland, Fla., I went out early one morning with Sparky Anderson. The manager wanted to look at some prospects working out on a practice field, across the way from Marchant Stadium. There were players from Latin America and visitors from Japan, and the scene evoked a luscious image for me:

"The mix of languages with the smell of orange blossoms

from a nearby grove is enchanting. Spring training can be at once hard and sweet, like rock candy."

A couple of years later, as spring training was about to begin, I offered this passage:

"Looking out the window today, there is only winter in Michigan. But knowing that pitchers and catchers begin workouts Tuesday in Lakeland gives us just a wee hint of better times. A tiny ray of sunshine jumping off the printed page.

"For those lucky enough to be able to get away, spring training is a time of renewal. Reunion. A chance to visit with your youth."

Readers in snowbound Michigan loved it. A week or so later, a couple who had recently arrived in Florida from Traverse City staked out the press box at Marchant Stadium just so they could meet me and tell me how much they liked that story.

Those hidden gems can sometimes move people that way. And they're great fun to write.

A Gentler Mike Tyson Gets Ready for Andrew Golota

By TIM DAHLBERG
AP Sports Writer

LAS VEGAS (AP)—Sitting on a bench in a shower room after four rounds of sparring, Mike Tyson seemed neither manic nor depressive. He didn't talk about eating Lennox Lewis' children or threaten to hurt anyone.

Instead, he chatted affably for about a half-hour, ignoring the running shower to talk about everything from wrestler Hulk Hogan to comedian Lenny Bruce.

The question inevitably arose: Was this version of Tyson for real?

"They did diagnose me stark raving mad," Tyson said, grinning.

If he was, he did a good job of hiding it in a gym near downtown where he sparred Friday for the last time before leaving for Detroit to fight Andrew Golota.

Unlike a similar session in May, when he was angered by a female photographer being in the gym, Tyson went out of his way to greet a reporter he had invited over and to offer an explanation of sorts for his bizarre behavior of recent months.

"You know, Lennox doesn't have any kids," Tyson said. "I knew that."

And his performance at a Los Angeles press conference last month where he climbed on a table, stripped off his shirt and talked about his sexual performance?

"Some of it you can believe," Tyson said, "and some is bull."

No wonder Tyson loves Hulk Hogan, Stone Cold Steve Austin and other professional wrestlers. He's made himself into a personality larger than anything the World Wrestling Federation can hope to create. And he realizes this—no one buys tickets to see a nice guy in the ring.

"I had no personality when I started fighting," Tyson said. "Now I do. There's nobody nicer than Evander (Holyfield), at face value that is. Nobody nicer than Lennox Lewis. But they can't sell tickets. I can."

Tyson's fight with Golota, set for Friday at The Palace in Auburn Hills, Mich., is something straight out of the WWF, matching the Foul Pole against Tyson, whose escapades keep getting stranger and stranger the longer he fights.

But the fact he sells tickets is evident in the pay-per-view price of $50, which is $5 more than Lewis and David Tua are charging for their Nov. 11 fight for the heavyweight title.

"This is a fight that is meant for me," Tyson said. "I'm excited about it."

Tyson's strategy is no different for Golota than anyone else. He's not worried about low blows ("They don't hurt if you have a cup") and doesn't think Golota brings anything to worry him in the ring.

Tyson took some punches during a sparring session Friday at the Golden Gloves gym, but was relentless as usual and ended the session early with a right hand to the body that put his opponent on his knees.

"I think Mike is a much better fighter than he was before," trainer Tommy Brooks said. "Before he just used to wing his shots. Now he's picking his spots."

Tyson wasn't so sure.

"I wish I felt as good as he says I look," he said.

Assuming he beats Golota, manager Shelly Finkel wants Tyson to fight Holyfield in what appears to be only one of two big money fights out there for the former champion.

That will have to happen without Don King, though, who promotes Holyfield. And that's not likely.

Tyson is still bitter toward King, whom he sued after breaking with him three years ago, claiming he stole $100 million of his earnings.

"He made millions of dollars from me and could have kept making them," Tyson said. "These people abused me. Not because they are smarter and better than me, but because I trusted them. I made a mistake, but I won't make another."

Even the thought of King wasn't enough, though, to get Tyson too excited. The shower was still running, and it was time to go.

But not without one last parting thought.

"I mix truth with lies," he said. "Some of it is a lot of fun."

Prep Football Mecca Tries to Deal With Loss of Longtime Coach

By PAUL NEWBERRY
AP Sports Writer

VALDOSTA, Ga. (AP)—A light rain falls as a hundred youngsters sprint up and down the field at the approach of another muggy south Georgia night.

This was the time of day when Nick Hyder would walk across the grass at the end of football practice, twirling his omnipresent whistle, dispensing the lessons of life underneath the giant water tower that proclaims this to be "Wildcat Country."

"Eat your breakfast!" he would yell. "Remember, we love ya!"

As Harvey Moore surveyed the end of Wednesday's practice, he couldn't help noticing what a quieter, sadder place Valdosta High School has become since Hyder's death 3½ months ago.

"It's really kind of strange not to see coach Hyder walking around out there," said Moore, who had two sons play for the Wildcats.

For 22 years, Hyder was a giant figure looming over one of the most famous high school football programs in the country. His teams won 249 games, lost only 36 and tied two. Seven times, they won the state championship. Three times, they claimed the mythical national title.

Yet he always insisted that football wasn't the most important thing in his life.

"God, family, country, academics, friends, Wildcats" were his priorities, in that order, and he preached them constantly to the young men who came into his life each year.

With no children of his own, Hyder became a father to thousands.

"I'll always remember the spiritual values he taught us, the things we could use not just on the football field, but in the classrooms, in the hallway," running back Marcus Ray said. "We've got other great coaches, but I don't know if we'll ever have another coach that preaches to us like coach Hyder did."

Hyder died suddenly May 16, the victim of a heart attack as he sat in the school lunchroom. At 61, he appeared to be the epitome of health. He had already scheduled offseason workouts for his players and was making plans to carry the Olympic torch when it came through Valdosta.

In these parts, it was akin to the day Bear Bryant died in Alabama.

"I just couldn't believe it," quarterback Dusty Bonner said. "I actually said to myself, 'Nick Hyder is not dead. That couldn't happen to him.' "

But it did. When they buried Hyder three days later, more than 7,000 people turned out at Cleveland Field in 96-degree heat to pay their final respects. Country-club regulars mixed with public housing tenants; white men in overalls stood side-by-side with black women carrying fans bearing the likeness of Martin Luther King Jr.

"Black, white, every kind of race came to see him, because he always talked with them," Bonner said.

Hyder was white, but he transcended color. Moore remembered telling Hyder that a black player's mother was sick. When Moore stopped by after practice, he found that the coach was already there to check on the family, he said.

Such stories are endless in this town of 40,000 that hugs the Florida border.

The day after the funeral, the players returned to the weight room to begin preparing for the new season, following the schedule that Hyder left for them. Over the summer, one of Hyder's players carried the Olympic torch in his place, with the rest of the team following behind.

That helped everyone deal with the grief, but the players got another jolt when they returned to practice and realized that Hyder wouldn't be there to help them prepare for Saturday's first game.

"I still expect to see him walk around the corner," Bonner said.

Hyder was replaced by Mike O'Brien, a quiet man with a cherubic face who served as an assistant for 15 years. The differences between the two are striking, despite their long-term association.

O'Brien is a coach. Hyder was a presence.

"He had a lot of little things he did, some that were real funny, some that were sort of irritating," O'Brien recalled. "He knew how to punch your buttons. He was a good head coach, he really was, and a very intense man.

"I'm very intense, but in a different kind of way. The kids have to learn to understand me. For instance, coach Hyder was a great speaker. He loved to talk and all that. I don't. The kids are having to get used to that, and they are."

Yes, football goes on at Valdosta High.

The 5-year-olds still head down to the Boys Club to don helmets and pads for the first time, already dreaming of the day when they can wear the black and gold Wildcats uniform.

On Friday nights, Cleveland Field will be packed with thousands of townsfolk, cheering on their beloved team. And by the end of the year, Valdosta likely will be in the running for another state championship.

That's they way Hyder would have wanted it, everyone agrees.

"I just know that every time we walk out there on that field, he'll be sitting up there watching," said Bonner, his voice choking with emotion. "He'll be sitting up there in heaven, probably saying, 'Oh, don't do that.'

"He'll be up there twirling that whistle."

From First Moment as Owner, Schott Was Unique

By JOE KAY
AP Sports Writer

CINCINNATI (AP)—From her first moments as owner of a major league team, Marge Schott made it clear she would do things her way.

Schott made her grand entrance as the new Cincinnati Reds owner on Dec. 21, 1984, by letting her St. Bernard lead the way into a crowded meeting room at Riverfront Stadium.

"Who else would walk in with a dog?" she proudly asked reporters.

Who else? That question would be asked again and again during Schott's 15-year reign as owner of baseball's first professional team.

Who else would chase away the team's scouts, complaining that all they do is watch baseball games?

Who else would refer to her general managers dismissively as "whatchamadoodle" and show little interest in learning the names of her players?

Who else would make her dogs the center of attention, allowing them the run of the field and the offices?

Who else would stubbornly refuse to curb her inflammatory comments, even after a suspension?

Only Marge Schott. And now, with baseball owners approving her sale to three limited partners Wednesday, the end of her news-making reign is at hand.

"I don't think she understood a lot of things," said Bob Howsam, who turned the club over to Schott. "She thought she did."

Howsam, who built the Big Red Machine of the 1970s, knew Schott from social occasions when she made an offer to buy the team from William and James Williams in 1984. At the time, she was known as a wealthy widow who made campy commercials for her car dealerships.

She calmed fears about her lack of baseball expertise by saying she'd leave decisions to those in the know. Howsam took her at her word and lobbied baseball to approve the sale.

Schott got the team. Howsam got a surprise.

"It turned out to be the worst thing I think I've ever done in baseball," Howsam said in a telephone interview.

Fans and the local media initially embraced the change from the publicity-shy Williams brothers to the front-and-center Schott. But right away, she dropped hints that things would work out much differently than everyone expected.

"They're private because they're smart," she said of the previous owners. "I'm public because I'm dumb."

Howsam retired as planned in 1985 and Schott moved into his office, dogs in tow. By that time, Howsam had gotten a glimpse of the problems ahead.

He heard her coarse language. He learned how little she thought of the farm system. He got in her doghouse by telling reporters the team was making money while she claimed it was losing millions.

He was taken aback when Schott rejected his offers to help her understand her new endeavor.

"I told her I would sit down and show her how baseball accounting was," Howsam said. "She said she didn't need any help. That was it."

Within two years, Schott had taken tight control of the team. Any purchase of $50 or more had to be approved by her. She got involved in player moves. She fought the team's limited partners.

She was becoming a different type of owner than anyone anticipated, and she made no apologies for her roughshod style.

"They never had a hands-on management before," she said. "You have to have that to keep track of what's going on."

Her methods alienated employees and resulted in an exodus of front-office officials and farm system personnel. The team's limited partners challenged Schott, hoping to rein her in and, ultimately, get her out. She survived the challenge and became more intractable.

For the most part, those festering problems remained a secondary matter while manager Pete Rose led the team to four consecutive second-place finishes. Schott was content letting Rose get most of the attention.

Once he was banned for life for gambling in 1989, Schott assumed a higher profile. She made her St. Bernard the focal point in 1990, rubbing dog hair on manager Lou Piniella for good luck.

Her team won the World Series with a homegrown roster that was in the pipeline before she began slashing the farm system. It was her finest moment as owner and brought her a lot of attention, but not enough to satisfy.

She complained that the other owners didn't dote on her enough during their next meeting, giving her roses and congratulations and then moving on to other matters.

"I didn't feel hurt but, being a woman, maybe I expected a little more attention," she said.

For the rest of her reign as owner, she never lacked attention.

Her treatment of the farm system in the 1980s caught up with the team in the '90s. The farm system produced little, forcing the small-market team to compete for free agents just as salaries were taking off.

By 1995, the Reds had the second-biggest payroll in the National League and one of the least-productive farm systems. The Reds made it to the NL championship series only to be swept by Atlanta, then began a retrenching that resulted in three years without a winning record.

Overshadowing all of it was Schott's public image. The '90 World Series championship gave her a forum; she used it to speak her mind about Hitler, minorities and a wide range of topics that had nothing to do with baseball.

Her use of racial and ethnic slurs was at the heart of a lawsuit by a fired employee and made baseball's treatment of minorities a national focal point in 1992. Baseball's executive council suspended her for the 1993 season, hoping it would send a message and teach her a lesson.

Nothing changed when she returned. She continued to do interviews that kept baseball on the defensive. In one, she suggested that Hitler was good in the beginning but just went too far. In another, she said racism was something created by the media.

"I don't think Marge has anything against any one group of people or race," Rose said. "I just don't think she likes anybody."

Baseball and the team's limited partners began exploring ways to muzzle her and force her out.

Faced with another suspension for inflammatory comments, Schott turned day-to-day decision-making over to managing executive John Allen in 1996. She was an owner in name only for the last few years, allowed input on the annual budget and negotiations for a new ballpark.

Allen reversed a lot of her decisions, began rebuilding the farm system and strengthening the threadbare front office. By 1999, the team was competing for the playoffs again.

In the meantime, the limited partners got some leverage. Their ownership agreement expired at the end of 2000, when they could oust Schott. With baseball hinting she should sell and the limited partners ready to get rid of her, Schott relented and made a deal with three of the limiteds.

The stormy Schott years were over.

"It's been very sad," Howsam said. "She really had the opportunity to do great things for Cincinnati baseball."

Assignments

1. Call for an appointment to visit the nearest AP bureau and talk to a sports writer, staffer, or bureau chief about local sports coverage, stories that are used on the national wire, and the details of their jobs.
2. Accompany an AP sports writer, if possible, to a game, observing everything from the pregame interviews to the postgame quotes and notes.
3. Check out all the sports events in your area in the upcoming week as if you were an AP sports writer, and make up a schedule of coverage for everything.

Columns

Once there was the Age of Reason. We live in the Age of Opinion, an age of sports columnists as multimedia stars (with books, radio and TV talk shows, and Web sites) who gain modest fame and fortune covering athletes, agents, owners, and others who are far more famous and fortunate.

Columnists live out a fan's fantasy, bouncing from sport to sport, playing down the fact that there's more to the job than kicking back after a game with a cold brew and musing in print or on the air about how swell it all was.

The best sports columnists make their jobs look easy. Their columns are silky, not strained, their ideas reflect a certain intelligence, and the jokes make people laugh. They are often the best reporters and best writers on the staff, people who paid their dues and showed their talent on beats and features. They are writers who found their voice and developed perspective, and they try to bring passion and energy to their

Fusaichi Pegasus, left, with jockey Kent Desormeaux aboard, crosses the finish line to win the 126th running of the Kentucky Derby at Churchill Downs, Saturday, May 6, 2000, in Louisville, Ky. Aptitude, right, with jockey Alex Solis up, finished in second. (AP Photo/Al Behrman)

work every day, turning out two, three, four or more columns a week.

As they watch the games and reflect on the issues of the hour, columnists confront a deflating paradox: Sport is essentially a frivolous endeavor, sometimes meaningless and inconsequential, and a columnist's life can be seen as the pursuit of the superficial and trivial. Luckily, that's not how it plays out. The writer and the reader often willingly suspend the truth about sport and choose to take it very seriously because that makes everybody happy. Sport is an escape from life and an embrace of living, and the tension between those two thoughts can produce exquisite drama or comedy. For the avid columnist and the rabid fan, there is nothing more serious than the games and the people who play them.

Columns come in a variety of sizes—from 700 to 1,200 words—and flavors: analytical, angry, breezy, comical, controversial, descriptive, evocative . . . on through the alphabet . . . indignant, ironic, irreverent, mournful, newsy, philosophical, poignant, scornful, and more, down to zingy.

At their best, they offer insight or humor about people playing games, the pleasure of a smile from poetic phrases and crystalline prose. They may be combative or wistful, essays or rants or tales of all sorts. They are sharp and true, nothing faked, each column as distinctive as the face above the words. Some are modern allegories, but the best stay away from preaching. They avoid the metaphor-and-microcosm-of-life stuff. They entertain, they teach, they make readers think. They provoke laughter and tears and terror. Sometimes they make readers want to rip up the paper and cancel the subscription—at least until the next column.

The biggest sin a sports columnist can commit is to be boring. That's closely related to another deadly sin: sloth. The best columnists get out and around. They go to games and locker rooms, talk to people in the hallways and make calls to find out more. They keep up with everything—sports, news, TV, movies. They read fiction and nonfiction. They know what's going on, have something to say about it, and can say it in their columns better than anyone else. How long does it take to write a column? It takes a lifetime.

In a game story, *Los Angeles Times* sports editor Bill Dwyre is looking for a writer who does more than regurgitate statistics or string together quotes. He wants to see writing that involves all the senses, writing that doesn't have horse blinders on it, writing that takes a chance, goes out on a limb, tries to be different. In a column, Dwyre says, all of that is multiplied five or six times.

"Then you've really got to have flair," he says. "Then you've got to have innovation and creativity. A columnist, more than anything else, needs a strength of ideas to start with. In a column, as opposed to a news story or even a feature, I need to feel the person's passion or anger. A column needs some emotion imparted."

It's no different at a smaller paper, where a columnist like the *Dayton Daily News*'s recently retired Gary Nuhn might wield even more clout in the community.

"Gary Nuhn was the guy who would ruffle feathers," *Daily News* sports editor Dean Rock says. "The guy had an edge to him, pissed off just about everyone in town for one reason or another. I think you need that commentary and a voice. I would like to have a columnist who can turn out a humorous piece, who can tell a story that will make you cry, and who can have an edge to him that will piss some people off. But it's hard to find those people."

For AP sports editor Terry Taylor, a columnist should have a distinctive voice and a point above all else, not be a feature writer in disguise.

"Columnists are entertainers, they're teachers, they tell you how to fix things," she says. "Columnists have more license and free rein on creativity than anybody else in the sports section. It's where your eyes go first when you pick up the paper, at least mine do. You want to know, 'What's he going to say today? Who's he going to throttle? What does he think about Bill Parcells?' You really want to know what they think, and then you decide whether you're going to agree with them or whether you think they're full of garbage."

Though many young sports writers aspire to become columnists, few will achieve the status of those whose work and thoughts are represented here: Dave Anderson, George Vecsey, and Ira Berkow of the *New York Times,* Bill Plaschke of the *Los Angeles Times,* Christine Brennan of *USA Today,* Bob Ryan of the *Boston Globe,* Jim Litke of The Associated Press, Michael Wilbon of the *Washington Post.*

They are among the best in the business, and what they have to say about reporting, research, interviewing, and style, as much as their views on columns, is relevant to anyone at any level in the sports writing game. They covered the beats, they paid their dues, and they are turning out some of the best writing on the sports pages.

A couple dozen others could just as easily have been included, among them Rick Reilly of *Sports Illustrated,* Mitch Albom of the *Detroit Free Press,* Mark Whicker of the *Orange County Register,* Bruce Jenkins of the *San Francisco Chronicle,* Harvey Araton and William Rhoden of the *New York Times,* Fred Klein of the *Wall Street Journal,* Filip Bondi and Mark Kriegel of the *New York Daily News,* Tony Kornheiser of the *Washington Post,* Mark Kram of the *Philadelphia Daily News.*

"There are hundreds of thousands of guys out there who can stand at the bar and pontificate," says Bob Ryan, who has heard his share of them. "They can sound pretty knowledgeable about sports. Some of them can even call up talk shows and express their viewpoint with some reasonable coherence. However, of those hundreds of thousands, probably only a few hundred could sit down and write anything that would make sense. Writing is not speaking. Writing is a whole other craft. If you don't have a love of language, if you don't get the little hairs up on the back of your neck when you read passages that soar, if you're not a literary person, then you can't be a great columnist. You can be an acceptable columnist, I guess, but you can't be a great one."

The great columnists of the past—Ring Lardner, Frank Graham, Red Smith, Jimmy Cannon, Bill Heinz, Jim Murray—created the modern form and served as models for many of today's best writers. I grew up reading Smith and Cannon, along with the *New York Post*'s Larry Merchant, Milton Gross, and my favorite for passion, color, and the dexterity

An LSU fan rides the goal post after LSU's upset victory over number one ranked Florida at Baton Rouge, La., Saturday, Oct. 11, 1997. LSU defeated the Florida Gators 28-21. (AP Photo/David Rae Morris)

to bounce between news and sports, Pete Hamill. They could stand shoulder to shoulder with any writer today and be better than most. Their columns should be read by every sports writer with a desire to see the possibilities a column holds. Smith's columns from half a century ago, for example, still sound fresh, despite all the changes in the sporting scene. Consider Smith's descriptive lead in a 1948 column titled "Rendezvous with Danger":

A fat, jovial man is sitting on the tailboard of a small enclosed truck inside the first turn of the Indianapolis Motor Speedway. His machine is four rows back from the rail, one among thousands and thousands of cars that stand, glittering under the sun, almost as far as the eye can see across this clamorous, hideous cauldron of noise and speed and reeking oil. On the truck's floor is a bed of straw with tangled blankets and mussed pillows. The man says he and two friends— "three bachelors from Gary"— drove over yesterday and pulled up in line maybe half a mile outside the gate about eight o'clock last night.

"How was the sleeping in here?"

"Fine. We had a great time. Left the truck in line and went into town and drank coffee all night. The line started moving in at five this morning. Have a can of beer?"

As good as Smith was with words, he always considered himself a reporter first and foremost. In this brief passage, so rich in detail that you can almost hear the noise and smell the oil, he demonstrates what distinguishes the best sports writers. They take you to the scene and make you feel it. Smith used his eyes and ears, and he listened closely to the way people spoke.

At his feet, a metal box holds beer cans in melting ice. He has a box of crackers open at his knees, a beer in his hand, and around him are paper parcels of food.

"You're pretty well stocked. Can you see the race from the truck top?"

"Not so good. We were over by that gate awhile. Couldn't see anything from there, either."

"Kind of a long drag, wasn't it,

waiting all night and not seeing much now?

"Yes, but it was worth it. Sure you won't have a beer?"

Smith goes on in this column to tell what happens in the race, but it is much more than an account of who won, who lost, and why. It is a column built on so many fine details and phrases that his own views slip in unobtrusively. The reader gets the idea that Smith is not fond of Indy's "monstrous holiday compounded of dust and danger and noise." He lets the reader know that the race itself is almost an afterthought, even for those who came to watch. But he lets the story unfold at an easy pace and delivers the goods at the end.

This particular area, where the infield crowds fight for position near the turn because the turns are the danger points in the annual five-hundred-mile race, offering the likeliest opportunity to see a man untidily killed, is an indescribable place, a grassy slum of gray squalor.

Here a fat woman in halter and shorts sits sunning herself on a camp stool. There a girl in slacks lies sprawled in sleep beneath a truck. The car tops are cluttered like windowsills along the Third Avenue El, covered with mattresses and blankets and seat cushions and homemade platforms supporting boxes, chairs, folding stools.

The car interiors have the homey, lived-in look of beds that haven't been made up for three days. Some have blankets or newspapers hung over windows and windshields for protection from the sun and a smidgen of privacy. The men are virtually all coatless, for it's a warmish day, and many are peeled to the waist. There's one shaving in front of his rear-view mirror. When a luggage compartment is opened, it generally reveals a washtub of iced beer.

There is a skeleton skyline of scaffolding, mostly unpainted two-by-fours set up astraddle the automobiles and supporting an observation platform perhaps fifteen feet high. Some are professional jobs of structural steel, bolted together and rising as high as twenty-five feet.

One of the tallest and certainly the most precarious looking consists of two double-length

A Nebraska fan celebrates as the Huskers enjoy a perfect season at the end of the Fiesta Bowl with Florida in Tempe, Ariz., Tuesday evening, Jan. 2, 1996. Nebraska beat Florida 62-24 to win the national collegiate title. (AP Photo/Jim Gerberich)

painters' ladders propped up in an inverted V. Two or three planks thrust between the upper rungs make unsteady perches against the sky.

The earth is a vast litter of crushed lunch boxes and tattered paper and beer cans and whiskey bottles and banana skins and orange peels and the heels of used sandwiches and blankets and rai-

ment and people. Over everything is the reek of burning castor oil, the incessant, nerve-shattering roar of racing motors.

This is the Indianapolis "500," a gigantic, grimy lawn party, a monstrous holiday compounded of dust and danger and noise, the world's biggest carnival midway and the closest sporting approach permitted by the Humane Society to the pastimes which once made the Roman Colosseum known as the Yankee Stadium of its day (cars are used in this entertainment because the S.P.C.A. frowns on lions).

The speedway is a rambling, ramshackle plant enclosed by two and a half miles of brick-paved track and the only space not jammed is the nine-hole golf course in the remotest part of the infield. Through binoculars from the press loft, couples can be seen reclining in comradely embrace beneath the trees on the links, but there seem to be no golfers.

It is said there are 175,000 people here, although gates started to close half an hour before race time. At that morning hour the Purdue University band was on the track giving brassy evidence of the advantages of higher education. At length these embryo Sammy Kayes tied into the national anthem and followed with "Taps," just in case. Bombs went off. Rockets burst in air, making a heavy flak pattern below cruising planes. James Melton sang "Back Home Again in Indiana" slowly, a full four seconds off the track record.

The cars had been pushed into place, three abreast in eleven ranks. Their drivers, goggled and helmeted, looked like Buck Rogers cutouts. The flying start was a burst of thunder, a blur of colors. Since then, it has been an unceasing grind, hour after hour, making the eyeballs ache, the temples throb. Every car has a different voice, none soothing. There is a twelve-cylinder Mercedes said to have been built for Adolf Hitler; it runs with a scream like Adolf's conscience.

Now, late in the race, the favored lane near the outside, which is called "the groove," has been blackened with oil. Coming down the straightaway, the cars skitter nervously on this slick, swinging their hips like Powers models. Most of the thirteen drivers still in the race steer to the cleaner bricks inside the strip.

Duke Nalon stays in the groove, though, and is leading with only fifteen of the two hundred laps remaining. He has the fastest, most powerful brute of a car ever put on this track, but its speed requires a special fuel which gives poor mileage, and now he pulls in for refueling. The crowd gives him a yell, the first time its voice has been heard all day. The pit crew works swiftly, finishes, can't get the motor started again. The car starts once, dies, and must be pushed back to the pit for more feverish seconds. This is the day's most exciting moment.

When Nalon finally goes away, to another small cheer, Mauri Rose and Bill Holland are ahead of him. The race is over; it was lost there at the gas pump.

Dave Anderson, who included that column in a compilation called *The Red Smith Reader* after Smith's death in 1982, zeros in on "big names, big games or big issues" in his own columns. A Pulitzer Prize winner like Smith, Anderson believes that people want to read, most of all, about people. Many of his columns have a casual, comfortable feel, and they convey a sense of knowledge and perspective.

Here is how some of his colleagues approach their columns.

George Vecsey: "I always have a motive in every column I do. There's some point I am trying to make or explain about something that has happened in the news. It might seem like I'm just telling a

story or talking about somebody, but I have chosen it for a reason. I think you can seduce the reader with words. It's harder to seduce an editor, in a sense, because they're looking for the angle, and the angle is kind of laid in there between the lines in a column. I'm telling a story and I have a moral."

Michael Wilbon: "I am a fan of great moments and human drama in athletic competition. As corny as that sounds, that's what I really feel passionate about. I try to tell the story of that to readers the next day. I try to get them to think about some point that they might not have considered. They may completely disagree with me when they pick up the column. I am trying to convince them to see it my way so they can relate to that fantastic story, that human drama."

Christine Brennan: "My columns tend to be about issues. Women's sports or misbehaving athletes or the baseball slugger who takes androstenedione. That stuff really appeals to me. I do love jumping into the fray, and that surprises me. I've always enjoyed a good argument, but I never necessarily did it with 3 million readers. So I'm kind of amazed in a fun way at where this has taken me. I wasn't expecting to pick fights or to cause trouble. That's not the goal. But if you're writing a negative column about the NFL and Ray Lewis, and how they're treating him, you know you're getting into it with the big boys."

Jim Litke: "Sometimes I'm taking people to task or explaining why someone would take one road as opposed to another. I try to stay close to the news, and that requires some reporting work as well. Something becomes an event because it has the news quality. It's poignant, it's funny, it's scary. Then I decide what my take on it is and I try to report it impartially and find out if my theory's any good. If it is, that's what I end up writing. If it's faulty, then I adjust it accordingly. It involves a little bit of detective work and a little bit of perspective work."

Oklahoma quarterback Josh Heupel, right, is congratulated as he walks off the field with the game ball after beating Florida State 13-2 in the Orange Bowl Wednesday, Jan. 3, 2001 at Pro Player Stadium in Miami, Fla. (AP Photo/David F. Martin)

Columns

Florida head coach Steve Spurrier gets drenched by offensive tackle Kenyatta Walker (78) as the Gators downed Auburn 28-6 in the SEC Championship at the Georgia Dome in Atlanta, Saturday, Dec. 2, 2000. (AP Photo/John Bazemore)

Ira Berkow: "If you're boring, you're dead. You have to make the reader interested, which means you have to use some element of entertainment. But that comes with good writing. You try to influence or persuade or make a point. You can't be too subtle, but you can't be too hard-hitting, either, because then you just turn off the people you are trying to influence. You have to have the facts. You can't be strictly emotional. There has to be some emotion in there, but you have to buttress the emotion with facts to make your point."

Bob Ryan: "A lot of columnists don't get what a column is, and basically what they write are thinly disguised features most of the time. You've got to take a stand on things. Over the course of the year you should have written a lot of columns off the bench because the live quality is expected. You should have written profiles that are reasonably enlightening, and you should have looked out for some oddities, smaller things that aren't being properly appreciated in high schools or lesser known sports. And you never write just for effect. I write angry columns to get people that I'm angry with or that have tested my patience or that I think are frauds. But I don't write things to provoke reader reaction. That's not my vision of being a columnist. I see a lot of columns that are just cheap tricks to get reaction. I can't do that. I have to live with it. I have to be able to defend it. Now if you can persuade me that I'm wrong, fine. Then I've got another column."

Some of the best sports columnists came out of the ranks of the news sections. They were hard-nosed reporters who, one fine spring day when the sound of fungoes filled the air, had an epiphany of sorts: Life truly is more fun in the sports department.

George Vecsey worked as a news reporter for 10 years, including a couple of years as *The New York Times*'s Appalachia national correspondent, starting in 1970. He moved from New York to Kentucky and covered coal mining, country music, and politics in half a dozen states. It was during that period that Vecsey coauthored *Loretta Lynn: Coal Miner's Daughter* with the singing star. Luck and persistence helped him break some big stories, Vecsey says modestly, and he took from his news experience the realization that a reporter has to be on the scene to do the job.

"I am not in the office much," Vecsey says. "All my instincts as a reporter, which I still think of myself as, means you've got to be in place. I am not a kid anymore, but I am blessed with being in good shape and I just love getting out and going to games. I went to an Islander hockey game the other night, and assistant coaches are asking, 'What are you doing out here?' It was kind of an ordinary night in the middle of winter. But you've got to get on it, got to show up. I am not just a big-event guy.

"I am a journalist and I am talking to fans, but I am not a fan. I'm in the locker room and I'm wandering around and I'm talking to ballplayers, so it gives me a different perspective. The fan doesn't know the players. He would like to, or thinks he'd like to, but I am there to set them straight, not to perpetuate myths or to root. I don't even care who wins. I want to know what the themes are coming into the game, what are the forces that are colliding, the good offense, the bad defense, the personalities of the people and the teams. It's my job to explain it all and what might happen. I don't try to say who's going to win. I'm a reporter, same as the people on the editorial page."

What else does it take to be an excellent columnist?

Bob Ryan: "A columnist really has to have something extra to bring to the table. You've got to have historical perspective, a frame of reference. You've got to have at least one sport, maybe two, where you really are an encyclopedia. I've got two. I don't make any claims for hockey and football, but I certainly will roll up my intellectual sleeves and say, 'Let's go, baby, I'll duke it out with you on baseball and basketball right here and now.' "

Christine Brennan: "I had 17 years of good, solid, hard reporting, just the facts, ma'am. Serious, interpretive journalism, investigative, everything. Even then it was a very big leap to become a columnist three years ago. I felt completely ready to do it, partially because I feel my opinions matter. We see a lot of people in our profession who, at age 25 or 27 or 30, get a column. They may be ready for it, but they may not be. I know I would not have been ready for it at that age. I needed to report. I needed to be at Super Bowls and be at Olympics and cover them and report and get to know people. Get to trust my own judgments and trust my own opinions. Not that I didn't have confidence, but you've just got to work your way through a lot to get to the point where you feel your opinion matters."

Ira Berkow: "You have to have an intellectual curiosity and a dis-

Florida State split end Robert Morgan (87) is unable to hold on to a pass in the end zone as Oklahoma's Derrick Strait (2) defends during the fourth quarter in the Orange Bowl, Wednesday, Jan. 3, 2001, at Pro Player Stadium in Miami, Fla. (AP Photo/David F. Martin)

tinctive voice. I would like to think that when I call somebody up, a friend of mine, I don't have to say, 'This is Ira,' because they recognize my voice. I would like to think that people could recognize my column, if you covered up my name . . . in the way I use language or maybe my view on things. A little twist here or there of irony or understatement. But the column is really an art form.

Not far from where I live there's a building in which there are very fine commercial artists, and on the building is written in script, 'Art is work.' I saw that the other day and I thought that was very good."

Michael Wilbon: "I believe in going to a lot of events. I know that these days a lot of columnists, a lot of famous columnists, don't go to games anymore. They don't leave their office. I don't believe in that. That is the only way to really get to know the people playing the games. This is not the '70s; you can't just call the PR guy to set up an interview. You don't have the great access that you once had with people in off-seasons. Now everybody's surrounded by agents and shoe reps and PR people and cousins and buddies, and it's not as easy to get access to the biggest and best stars in the athletic world anymore. You can do that if you go to games. You can't get to know Tiger Woods at a major, but you might be able to get him if you go to some smaller event. I got to know Michael Jordan by going to games in Indianapolis and Cleveland and Charlotte in December and January and February. I think columnists should do some reporting. Otherwise why is one columnist's opinion better than another's? That's a big deal to me. I'm not giving you something stale. My thing is to know that, being there and meeting these people, I am going to get more information and better information than the people that weren't there. I am not that big into entertainment. I'm partnered at the *Washington Post* with the most entertaining columnist in America, Tony Kornheiser, and I am not as funny as he is. I don't think anybody is in print. I'm trying to convince you to believe what I think. I am trying to provoke some thought and discussion about something that is either a hot-button issue or something you didn't even know about."

Jim Litke: "The true secret to column writing is flexibility. If you're writing about an event that happens in short, fast bursts, then you want to write short, fast sentences. Sentences that don't stop you at all. Boom, boom, boom, boom, boom. And move down the story real quick. If it's a story that involves a little more thought, and you're trying to lead somebody, as though you were making an argument, then you tend to write it more like an essayist than like a news guy. If you're trying to make fun of somebody, then you might mix three or four different styles and go for logical absurdity. The true secret of being a columnist vs. being a beat guy or any other guy in the newspaper is that you can take any event as it is and find a style that will give both information and a certain amount of perspective. Some are long on information and short on perspective, some are the other way around. But the point is, events happen differently and have different rhythms, and they probably mean different things at the end of the day."

At the end of the day, sports columnists are measured in equal parts by their readers and themselves. They create their own standards and try to live up to them each time they write. Some manage a home run once a week, some two or three times in a very good week. Bob Ryan says his minimum standard is "a standup double."

"The worst I want to feel about what I do on a consistent basis is what I call a Tony Perez double," Ryan says. "A one-hopper up against the wall, pull into second without a huff and a puff—a standup double. If I can't at least give you a standup double then I have failed. There's no way that anybody can hit one out of the park every day."

A sports columnist's life, even more than a beat writer's, is to be envied and pitied. At the top ranks, it is a seemingly glamorous life that offers front-row seats to games around the world, passes to all the locker rooms, free meals at gourmet restaurants, suites at posh hotels, a zillion frequent flier miles, and a laptop computer to tap out columns anytime, anywhere. Columnists at smaller papers, from the *Kalamazoo Gazette* to the *Everett Herald,* have their own share of privilege and power. They are the voices of their sports pages and their communities, and everybody in town knows who they are.

But consider the downside. Front-row seats come at the cost of cranking out artful columns in cold, cramped press boxes while fans are already snug in their beds.

Michael Johnson of the United States celebrates after he won the men's 200-meter final in a world record time of 19.32 at the 1996 Summer Olympic Games in Atlanta, Thursday, Aug. 1, 1996. (AP Photo/Doug Mills)

Locker room passes mean talking to dripping, naked athletes toweling off after a shower and wishing you would get out of their faces. Dining out means rarely eating at home, just as flying first-class means taking off on another lonely trip away from the family. Working anytime often translates into working all the time. A columnist's life is ruled by the column.

"As soon as you finish one column," Dave Anderson says, "you think, 'God, what am I gonna write for the next column?' "

Neither Anderson nor anyone else lucky enough to have this sweet a gig is asking for the slightest bit of sympathy. As Litke says when asked if he's happy with his career: "Frighteningly so."

For Christine Brennan, who has written two best-sellers on figure skating and appears frequently on television as a guest commentator, life doesn't get any better.

"This job is the greatest adventure," Brennan says. "I have gone around the world several times covering sports for a living. I can't believe that I do this. It's like, pinch me, this is really happening? It's not just an opportunity to write and create controversy at times or address issues and make people think about things. It's the adventure of it all from a purely personal standpoint, the people I meet and the things I've seen all through my love of journalism. I'm the luckiest person in the world. I just cannot imagine anything greater than this."

An American in Paris Rubs Some French the Wrong Way

By JIM LITKE
AP Sports Writer

PARIS (AP)—For all the ugly, hurtful things the French newspapers said about Lance Armstrong, their real sin was believing they could rattle him. Someone who has outraced cancer, after all, is hardly going to be stopped by bad reviews.

The 19th and next-to-last stage of the Tour de France ended Saturday afternoon some 220 miles from Paris, beneath bright skies at a science-fiction theme park called Futuroscope. It ended with Armstrong winning his fourth stage, probably the sweetest yet, since he got to walk off the podium with the leader's yellow jersey—*le maillot jaune*—still on his back and an arm draped over the shoulder of his just-arrived mother.

"It feels very special," he said afterward, speaking in French. "I wanted to show why I had the yellow jersey."

The win gave Armstrong a 7-minute, 37-second lead over his closest pursuer, Alex Zulle of Switzerland. Barring a crash or some other disaster Sunday, he will roll into Paris about 4 P.M. local time, zoom around the Arc de Triomphe, then up and down the wide boulevard of the Champs-Élysées to become only the second American to win the world's greatest bicycle race.

Armstrong's recovery from a deadly form of testicular cancer should be one of the best, most joyous comeback stories ever. Just 2½ years ago, after the disease had spread to his lungs and brain, doctors doubted Armstrong would live, let alone recover and compete in anything more strenuous than gin rummy.

But ever since he took control of the race, it has bothered some Frenchmen to no end that Armstrong was poised to win the event that defines, above all others, sport in their land. And not just because he's an American.

Armstrong's countryman, Greg LeMond, won here three times and is still widely adored. But LeMond's family bloodline traces back to France, where the Tour originated in 1903. And when he won the first time, in 1986, LeMond rode for a French team, and then for Belgian teams in his 1989 and 1990 victories.

One problem for Armstrong is that he's about to win the 2,306-mile, three-week-long race at a time when the Tour is itself recovering from a drug scandal that rocked the sport. Another is that for the first time since 1926, a Frenchman will not win even one stage of a race they've won a record 36 times—but not since 1985. And to top it off, Armstrong comes off sometimes as American as American gets.

He can be blunt where LeMond was boyish, he hails from big, bad Texas where

LeMond hails from frozen, friendly Minnesota. Worst of all, Armstrong rides for an American team. To let folks back home know how improbable a victory by an American team rider seems, U.S. Postal Service team manager Mark Gorski compared it to a French team crossing the Atlantic to win the Super Bowl.

The strange thing is that Armstrong's opening-stage win was greeted with relief. Trying to shake the specter of doping, promoters dubbed this year the "Tour of Redemption." And as a cancer survivor with no drug allegations clouding his past, Armstrong became their poster boy.

There was no grumbling when he won Stages 1 and 9, both time trials over flat courses, because Armstrong was the road-racing world champion in 1993. But French newspapers fired up the rumor mill on July 13, when he locked up the race with an uncharacteristically brilliant ride up into the Alps in Stage 10, and haven't shut it down since.

The surprising thing is how little venom has spilled over into the public. Already a hero in the United States, people riding bikes around Paris who are stopped for interviews refer to Armstrong as *"le miraculeux"*—the miraculous one—and a source of inspiration.

On the other hand, it's not hard to see where the suspicions spring from.

Until this year, Armstrong wasn't known as a strong mountain racer, a necessary component to be the overall Tour champion. But he came to France in the wet and cold of last winter to practice every stage, including the Alps, applying the same maniacal work ethic that sur-

prised his stateside doctors during an arduous recovery.

French newspapers, though, ignored that, instead suggesting that cycling had returned to doping as usual. The tone of the coverage shifted 180 degrees.

L'Equipe, the national sports daily, headlined its story "On Another Planet." The popular tabloid, *France Soir,* referred to him as "Stupefying Armstrong." They were double-entendres, but the newspapers' underlying message was clear: They suspected him of using performance-enhancing drugs.

The episode reached a crescendo when the respected daily, *LeMonde,* joined in. Saying it had copies of Armstrong's drug tests from the first two days of the race, it accused him of taking a banned medication. As it turned out, Armstrong had used a skin cream for his saddle sores that contained glucocorticoid, an anti-inflammatory steroid commonly used to treat rashes. It had nothing to do with performance enhancement and besides, the International Cycling Union noted Armstrong had a prescription to use it.

At a televised news conference Wednesday, Armstrong took no delight in being right. Instead, his demeanor went from blunt to bitter.

"They say stress causes cancer," he said. "So if you want to avoid cancer, don't come to the Tour de France and wear the yellow jersey. It's too much stress."

Yet, he's moved on from there faster than the newspapers, faster than the innuendo and whispers, too fast for anything or anybody but the winged goddess of victory to lay a hand on him.

Sports of The Times
The Old Dodger Dread Resurfaces

By GEORGE VECSEY
The New York Times

Dread and foreboding fill the air. They really are going to play this Subway Series, aren't they? But why this sudden gloom, this morbid sense that things are not right in the universe?

At first, I thought it was pure animal fear on my part. I had this awful premonition of vigilante mobs running amok in New York, speaking gibberish, frightening the populace. And that was just the news media.

But, no, there was another reason I did not want a Subway Series in my hometown.

"Cool it," younger colleagues told me. "It's going to be an event of a lifetime. Besides, you had a bunch of Subway Series when you were a kid. Let the rest of us have one."

Then I plumbed the depths of my emotions, and discovered the source of my pain. For weeks, I have been having this recurrent nightmare of a skinny man with a No. 1 on his back making a swooping catch of a wayward pop fly. Something bad is about to happen all over again.

You see, doctor, I carry around in my twitchy Subconscious a sports version of post-trauma depression. I do not want to relive the experience all over again. I do not want to root.

Mayors can root. There was Rudolph W. Giuliani in the Yankee clubhouse on Tuesday night (enduring a Champagne shower from his own male progeny, young Andrew) and proclaiming that while he is Mayor to all New York baseball teams, he could not help rooting for his childhood team, and therefore was picking the Yankees to win in six games.

Rooting is totally unprofessional from a sports columnist. Besides, how could anybody root against these Yankees of Bernie and El Duque and Paulie and other such compelling dudes? However, I have discovered, to my chagrin, that the reason I fear a Subway Series is that in my wayward youth I rooted for a team from Brooklyn. The Dodgers were a wonderful team. They were the first major league team to employ African-American players. They were a grand collection of individuals. They resided in a teeming little bandbox often chock-full of eccentrics. And they could play.

They could play in April. They could play in May. They could play in June. They could play in July. They could play in August. They could play in September. In fact, they were so skilled in the warmer months that Roger Kahn wrote one of the classic sports books called *The Boys of Summer.*

It was autumn that was the problem.

When I was a lad, terrible things happened to the Brooklyn Dodgers in October. These flashbacks keep invading my brain. I see a relief pitcher named Joe Page hopping over the bullpen fence and throwing five—five!—scoreless innings in the seventh game of the 1947 World Series.

I see Tommy Henrich slugging a home run off Don Newcombe to end the first game of the 1949 World Series. Nearly half a century later, Steve Jacobson, that exceptional sports columnist for *Newsday,* lamented to Henrich that he had been unable to study because of the home run.

"Tough," Henrich retorted. "What were you going to be, a doctor?"

Our lives were affected by these awful events. Dodgers fans remember Bobby Thomson's homer that won the 1951 playoff while Giants fans still mourn the fortuitous rainout that allowed the Yankees to regroup during the World Series. In 1952, there was Billy Martin's dashing catch of Jackie Robinson's pop-up. The same scrawny second baseman, the aforementioned No. 1, batted .500 against the Dodgers in 1953. In 1955, the Dodgers temporarily got things right, but in 1956, Yogi Berra hit three homers off Newcombe, and things were pretty much back to normal.

That is ancient history, but it lives today, like a Love Canal with a 1,000-year life. The Mets are the spiritual heirs of the Dodgers and the Giants. There are certain ions spinning around in the atmosphere. We are what we eat. Karma returns.

The Yankees of old were always under a dark cloud, just like this aging lot. Poor old DiMaggio had a bad heel, or star-crossed Mantle had bad knees, or some other Yankee star had the chilblains. Whatever. The real damage always came from the Yankees you were not watching closely, the Martins and the Mizes, the Kuckses and the Kuzavas.

It's all coming back to me now, doctor. The cold sweats. On Tuesday night, with the Yankees in trouble, somebody hit a grounder up the middle. The ball rolled up Derek Jeter's arm, a total clown play, the kind that could wreck an entire season for any other franchise, but instead the ball floated directly to Luis Sojo, the well-traveled Yankee, now filling in admirably on defense for the befuddled Chuck Knoblauch.

And there, doctor, just as it recurs in my haunted sleep cycles, was Luis Sojo, in the right place at the right time, just like Billy Martin in the bad old days, hauling it in for the force play that essentially killed the rally. Those things were always happening to my Dodgers, doctor. I want to know why.

The Mets just might be the best team in baseball right now. They can take care of themselves. But this Subway Series raises old psychic wounds. We are reminded of Yankee power and Yankee pride and Yankee ingenuity and, most of all, we are reminded of Yankee luck. It's not that I root, doctor, but this Subway Series fills me with fear and trembling.

Iverson's Bad Rap Is Well-Deserved

By Michael Wilbon
Washington Post

Like a lot of other folks who care about basketball, I keep waiting for Allen Iverson to grow up. I keep waiting for him to lift some weights and get stronger so that he can better withstand the pounding he takes. I keep waiting, hoping for him to realize that games are often won at the previous day's practice, which he may not have attended. I keep hoping that he is old enough now—25—to understand there's a world of difference between being a great talent and a great player, between somebody who's got game and a champion. I keep waiting for Iverson to understand that the notion of being a role model goes way beyond a lot of people walking around town wearing your jersey.

But here we are, at the start of NBA season No. 5, and Iverson seems no closer to getting any of this than he did four years ago. Maybe he's further away. My vigil appears to be in vain.

NBA camps have just opened, and Iverson is in the news already, again for the wrong reasons. The story with sizzle is the controversy over a soon-to-be-released rap CD on which Iverson does what the majority of thug rappers do: He demonstrates that he, too, can bash gays, degrade women and talk about shooting somebody. That's the genre. It's pretty clear how this breaks down; if you're under 30 (regardless of race, nationality, sex),

chances are overwhelming you're a lot more open to thug rap than if you're over 40. I'm 41, and most rap doesn't speak to me, doesn't move me whatsoever. But I do listen to it enough to know the lyrics Iverson's spewing on "Non-Fiction" are fairly common.

That doesn't mean people won't be offended, and legitimately so. Iverson's rap on gays, as reported earlier this week in the *Philadelphia Inquirer:* "Come to me with faggot tendencies/You'll be sleepin' where the maggots be." He also raps, "Man enough to pull a gun/Be man enough to squeeze it."

This is a young man who in the same breath will tell you he is a role model? Sadly, he is probably right on the mark. And sadly, the hip-hop community seems to get a pass on gay-bashing and misogynist behavior.

Given what this kid has been through in his life, and that the present environment existed long before he came along, many of us have extended Iverson the benefit of the doubt. He's about used it up. It's not about his twisted lyrics, specifically. It's about squandering talent, it's about being a self-absorbed egomaniac whose position in the culture isn't nearly as big as he thinks it is. It's about never listening to anyone, and having no regard for anything that doesn't revolve around him and his. Kinda like the very dead Notorious B.I.G. and Tupac, which I'm sure Iverson would take as a compliment.

I thought Iverson was getting somewhere when he said earlier this week, "The whole time I've been in the NBA, I haven't been professional at all. I always looked at it like it was just basketball. This year will definitely be the best season I've had since I've been in the NBA. I owe it to myself and my family and my teammates to be a better player.

"I'm concentrating on basketball. I haven't been working on my game as serious as I should've. I have the raw talent. This is going to be the most important year of my career because all eyes are on me this year. Everybody's wanting to see if I can be the captain, if I can be a leader, if I can be professional besides playing basketball, and if I'm up to the challenge. I'm ready for it because it's something I can do."

But the longer you listen to Iverson, the more you realize he's disconnected from the world we live in, even the world he lives in. The attitude is: I can be late or miss practice whenever I want because I'm Allen Iverson, The Answer, and the team don't have nothin' if it ain't got me. And if you make a big deal out of me cussin' the coach and standing up my teammates and getting fined 50 times in one season, then you must be a punk 'cause I'm tough and you ain't.

Iverson is ticked off because the 76ers tried to trade him because he repeatedly is late to practice, if he shows at all. You know what his take is?

"That's embarrassing to hear that an organization is thinking about trading its franchise player because he's tardy to practice."

Of course, it never occurred to him that it ought to be embarrassing for the franchise player to be tardy repeatedly. That wouldn't cross his mind. "You're going to send me to the worst team in the league?" he asked, incredulous at the possibility of going to the Los Angeles Clippers, apparently unaware that players a whole lot more accomplished than he is (Wilt and Kareem to name two) were traded in their prime.

Truth be told, the Clippers don't want Iverson. Several teams have turned down the chance to trade for him and here's why: They're afraid he'll never get with the program—anybody's program. He plays his heart out every time he puts on a uniform. For those 48 minutes, there isn't anything he won't do to win a basketball game. He'll sacrifice his body, he'll do the dirty work some superstars don't want to do. But the great players in any sport know it only starts there. And that's what Iverson hasn't grasped. You know what he said this week about his repeated tardiness, which by the way has angered his teammates?

"Yeah, I was late to practice, but, believe me, [the number of] times that I heard, nobody would put up with that. I'm not even brave enough to miss that many practices."

So how many, Allen? "I don't know; I wasn't counting. Don't nobody complain about the effort I give in a game. [Given the injuries and pounding he takes] it's bad enough I had to come to the game."

Iverson went on to say he was "hurt hearing some of the things the fans were saying, some of the things people on the coaching staff were saying. I thought a lot of people in this organization were my friends and I found out the hard way that there's no friends in this business besides your teammates."

I guess those would be the teammates for whom he won't come to practice on time. I guess those would be the friends who have begged him for years to get his act together, to try to realize there are obligations that come with an $80 million contract. If they're not sucking up to him, they're against him, they don't understand him, they're not as tough as he is.

Folks under 30 are tired of people my age wanting Iverson to be Bird or Magic or Jordan, and that's understandable. Differ-

ent time, different place, the world evolves. But I'm looking at Kevin Garnett now, at Ray Allen, at Tim Duncan, at Shaq and Kobe Bryant. There is a new generation of players trying to be all they can be. And they have fully developed lives outside of basketball.

Iverson, meanwhile, raps one thing, but his actions speak even louder. It's everybody else's fault, it's the coach's fault, it's the system's fault. He says he is going to change. It reminds me of Bob Knight saying he was going to change. I'm hoping Iverson is different because he's more than 30 years younger than Knight; he can grow up if he wants. But maybe it's more important for him to talk loud while saying nothing.

Cesspool Stinks? Shocking

BY BOB RYAN
BOSTON GLOBE *STAFF*

Is it possible to make a farce out of a farce?

Perhaps Molière himself could. While history reveals nothing to us about the great French playwright's view of sport, we might properly assume that even M. Molière could never have concocted anything as whimsical as a sub-headline appearing in the *Sunday Globe*. Perhaps you missed it.

SOUR ON THE SWEET SCIENCE
Golota actions blow to boxing

Huh?

Blow to boxing?

Next they'll be telling us lying is bad for politics.

Blow to boxing?

This just in: A double cheeseburger, an order of fries, and a vanilla shake do not constitute a health-food lunch.

Something—anything—a blow to boxing? That's like saying that nudity is an impediment to sex.

Boxing is, and just about always has been, beyond parody. To enjoy boxing is to make an intellectual pact with the sporting devil. Boxing wouldn't be boxing if it weren't rife with fraud, deceit, and wanton brutality. "Sweet science"? Nice try. How about "legalized brutality"?

The Mike Tyson–Andrew Golota bout was only the latest in a string of Tyson absurdities, the difference being that this time the other guy was even crazier than he is. Was/is Andrew Golota seriously injured, as we were told? Who knows? We were told that a Dr. Wesley Yapor, said to be a neurosurgeon at Chicago's Resurrection Medical Center, had diagnosed the man known as the "Foul Pole" with sustained disk problems that will require an operation. We were further told that Golota had additional injuries to his head (concussion) and face (fractured cheekbone). But I am shocked—shocked—that the injured warrior is already out of the hospital.

What was Tyson-Golota other than a ghoulish exhibition in the first place? The fight wasn't made because someone honestly believed it to be a worthy match of legitimate heavyweight title aspirants. Golota is known only for starting fights with known fighters, not for finishing any of them, and certainly not for winning any. The match was made in the hopes that all Marquis of Queensberry rules would be violated—by both men. Every reputable boxing analyst expected Tyson to pummel Golota. What the promoters fervently hoped was that before he did, something outrageous would happen.

There is no need to catalogue Tyson's sorry recent resume. He is a sad joke of a human being. That he happens to remain a viable contender is testimony to the quality of the modern heavyweight division, not to Tyson's actual level of current competence.

In a better world, the match would never have been made. In the off-center world of boxing, it was a natural.

But what's new? Boxing has been a source of amusement and/or embarrassment to civilized society for at least two centuries. It is base and it is brutal, and it has always been susceptible to cynical manipulation.

Does any of the following ring any bells?

Jack Johnson, supposedly lying on his back after a Jess Willard knockout punch, shading his eyes from the sun during a 1915 title bout in Havana.

Jack Dempsey destroying the same Jess Willard for the title on July 4, 1919, amid suggestions that he had worn gloves laden with, shall we say, lethal weaponry.

The pathetic saga of guileless Primo Carnera, a.k.a. "The Ambling Alp," who was allowed to think he had won the heavyweight title on the up-and-up in 1933, when, in fact, he had defeated a succession of dumpers, and whose plight was brilliantly fictionalized by Budd Schulberg in *The Harder They Fall.*

Jake LaMotta admitting he had thrown a fight, under orders, with the promise that in so doing he would be granted a title shot.

The mob's manipulation of boxing in the '40s and '50s under the guise of the International Boxing Club.

Mobbed-up Sonny Liston's two laughable fights against Cassius Clay/Muhammad Ali, quitting on the stool in the first and then being knocked out by—let's get serious—the bogus "Anchor Punch" in the second.

Outrageous judging decision after outrageous judging decision for the last century, most of them leaving us but one conclusion: The fix was in.

But the dishonesty and chicanery seemingly endemic to the game can sometimes be laughed at. Don King, who did serious time for manslaughter (to his credit, he never denied guilt), is so over-the-top full of, um, blarney that he has made himself into some sort of bizarre avuncular figure. Indeed, he and his hair are among the most recognizable artifacts in Western society, with most people not realizing that when he hasn't been hyping fights he's been busy diverting funds from hapless fighters into his own bank accounts. Such is the force of his personality that more people view him as harmless comic relief rather than the vicious and evil man he is.

Don King is a perfect metaphor for boxing.

Even if boxing were smoothly and properly administrated, boxing would still be boxing. Someone is always going to get hurt, and some of the hurt is even fatal. The latest reminder is lying in New England Medical Center.

His name is Bobby Tomasello, who entered the ring at the Roxy last Friday night full of youthful vigor and is fighting for his life after sustaining a blood clot in the brain during his fight with Steve Dotse.

Boxing's adherents tell us that it is the supreme test of manhood, and no one will argue that. Some call it the "hurting business," and again there is no argument. Boxing is not for wusses.

But is all this any reason why civilized society should lend this enterprise its seal of approval? Isn't there another less debilitating way to demonstrate virility (or, in the case of the strange women now in the game, femininity)?

The lucky few get rich and survive with all their faculties. Some survive with all their faculties, minus the riches. The majority emerge with neither money nor their health. And no one cares.

This is not a call to abolish boxing. That would only drive it underground and make it even more unsafe than it already is. All anyone can ask for is strict government supervision, the implementation of Olympic-style headgear—talk about dreaming—the elimination of all unsavory elements—even more dreaming—and, in general, the birth of an entirely new climate that would so homogenize it that perhaps it would cease to have an appeal and die a natural sporting death.

You want to hurt this sport? Clean it up completely. Now that would be a blow to boxing.

Women Athletes Need to Keep Their Clothes On

Christine Brennan
USA Today

INDIANAPOLIS—Here's my theory on women athletes: As they become more successful, they tend to get more forgetful.

As proof, let's look at the latest issue of *Sports Illustrated.* In the magazine, there's a full-page picture of Jenny Thompson, one of the world's greatest swimmers, standing on a beach in Northern California.

She remembered to wear her funky red boots. She remembered to wear the bottom part of her bathing suit.

But she forgot to wear the top.

Thompson, a shy, 27-year-old New Englander who always has been the epitome of Yankee modesty, is wearing nothing above her waist. She is officially topless. She is, however, clenching two well-placed fists.

Once upon a time, when athletes achieved great fame, they looked into a television camera and shouted that they were going to Disney World.

Now, more and more, women athletes in Olympic sports gaze into the lens of a photographer's camera and take off their clothes.

If undressing were a medal sport at the upcoming Sydney Olympic Games, the Americans would be favored to win the gold. Australia would give us a run for our money with their women's soccer team and its revealing calendar.

But look at the firepower we could throw at the Aussies: We'd have a dozen U.S. track and field athletes who posed in various stages of undress for a calendar of their own. We'd have Brandi Chastain posing with that strategically placed soccer ball in *Gear* magazine last year. And we'd have our swimmers. Not only Thompson in SI, but Dara Torres, Amy Van Dyken, Angel Martino and Thompson, all together in the altogether in *Women's Sports and Fitness* magazine. The four veteran sprint stars are standing in the shower area of the locker room at Stanford, apparently wearing nothing, seductively draped in one big American-flag towel.

Of all these photos, Thompson's SI pose is the one that's going to reach the most American households. It's the one that's already being discussed (wink-wink) on the pool deck at the U.S. Olympic swimming trials. It's the one that has parents' eyes popping in the natatorium lobby.

If I were Jenny Thompson, I'd start running around the country, buying up, oh, say, a couple million copies of the magazine. I say this because, while Thompson defends the picture as being a positive image for girls of a "strong . . . muscular" woman, I conducted my own informal poll during the weekend at the Olympic trials and discovered an entirely different opinion.

"For people looking up to her, it damages her image," said 17-year-old backstroker Suzanne Souders of Fort Lauderdale, Fla.

"I didn't think she'd do that," said a teenage girl who asked that her name not be used because she's been to Thompson's swimming camp.

"There's no reason for her to do that," said swimming parent Jean Short of San Jose, Calif. "She's No. 1 in the eyes of people. It just demeans yourself to do that."

"Why?" asked swimming legend and women's sports leader Donna de Varona. "Why do that? I guess I'm old-fashioned. I want them to keep their clothes on."

So do I. What's troubling about this trend is that there seems to be a warped attitude among some female athletes that it's not only proper to take off your clothes for a

picture, it's actually liberating. To them, it has become a kind of hyper-feminist act: Now that they've made it, they can take it all off.

"I'm proud of my body and the work that I've done to get it where it is," Thompson said.

Great. Then put on a tank top and strike a pose to show off those biceps. Wear a bathing suit while bench-pressing your boyfriend. Turn around and display your industrial-strength back as you did in an acclaimed print ad a couple of years ago.

By posing topless with her hands covering her breasts, Thompson doesn't send girls a message of empowerment. She instead sends them the insecure message that an old stereotype still lives and thrives.

If you doubt this, look at the picture and notice where your eye goes first. Not to those amazing legs or arms. Not to Thompson's all-American face. Not to her chiseled stomach.

No, right to her chest.

Assignments

1. Write an 800-word column before a college or pro game and sub out the lead or rewrite it within an hour after the game ends.

2. Pick up three columns over the Internet on the same subject and compare them in an 800-word critique. Which did you like best and why? Which was the most informative, the most enjoyable to read, and why? What bothered you about the column you liked least?

3. Write two columns in two different styles, one perhaps light and comical, the other more serious and combative.

Playing the Game

Long before I became a sports writer, I learned two lessons that have served me well throughout my career. One came in 10th grade when I confidently bet a friend that the skinny young braggart Cassius Clay couldn't possibly beat big, mean Sonny Liston. That lesson cost me only $25 and probably saved me thousands over the years as I realized that neither I nor the experts who made Liston an 8-1 favorite knew what we were talking about. If Clay could beat Liston, anything could happen, and I'd be wise to save my money rather than risk it on more foolish bets—and to refrain from predicting winners in stories.

The second lesson came a bit later when I learned to play chess, a game that entranced me with its leaping knights, slashing bishops, powerful queens, and limitless possibilities. I studied at a chess club, paid my dues to the street hustlers playing with timers at the granite tables in New York's Washington Square Park, and became good enough

Lisa Leslie of the United States battles Poland's Dorota Bukowska for a loose ball during the second half of a women's Group B Olympic basketball game in Sydney, Sunday, Sept. 24, 2000. The U.S. team won 76-57. (AP Photo/Roberto Borea)

to know with absolute certainty that there were worlds of moves and combinations I would never grasp, much less master. Bobby Fischer I wasn't. But along with that depressing insight came another, more useful, thought: If I *were* Bobby Fischer, I could escape virtually any threat, solve any problem, and find a way to win.

I've taken that attitude with me into the sports writing game. If I run into a jam, can't find somebody or some piece of information, I say to myself that there must be a way to do it. Be Bobby Fischer. Find a way out. Find a way to win.

In pursuit of a story, no matter whether it's for the *Lansing State Journal,* the *Los Angeles Times,* or The Associated Press, a reporter should be able to find anyone. All it takes is ingenuity and persistence, a refusal to be deterred by busy signals, wrong numbers, message machines, unanswered calls, or protective secretaries. You keep trying until you get through, even if it takes 50 calls to the same number. Sometimes you get lucky and the people you want to reach answer their

phones right away and tell you everything you want to know. Sometimes you make 10 calls in the morning, starting with East Coast numbers and working your way west because of the time zones, and don't get anyone. That's OK. It's like dropping your fishing line and waiting for a nibble. At some point, usually while you're trying to grab a sandwich, the fish bite and the calls come in. Quite often, two or three of the people you were trying to reach will call back at the same time, and you wind up juggling them.

This is the most basic form of research at any level: simply going after a story by calling people. Get their numbers from 411, telephone books, the Internet, disk directories, reverse directories, team or league guides, flacks, agents, friends, friends of friends, relatives, anyone who might be helpful. The Internet has expanded the power reporters have in tracking down people, but it is still just one tool, a supplement, not a substitute, for all the other tools available.

I often ask athletes and coaches for home phone numbers. I keep

Uruguay's Henry Gramajo and his horse Potencial fly over the Darug Bulada jump during the cross-country test for the Individual Three-Day Event at the Olympics at the Sydney International Equestrian Center at Horsley Park, Thursday, Sept. 21, 2000. The combination was eliminated from the competition after the jump. (AP Photo/Susan Walsh)

Russia's Viatcheslav Gorpichine, left, and his teammate Serguei Pogorelo, right, block Dragan Skrbic, centre, captain of Yugoslavia, during the Olympic men's handball semifinals game in Sydney, Friday, Sept. 29, 2000. Russia defeated Yugoslavia 29-26. (AP Photo/Themba Hadebe)

those numbers confidential and don't call unless it is important. Sometimes I've had to call people to check out rumors that they died. When they answer the phone, I know the rumor is wrong. Jack Dempsey was rumored to have died six times before he actually did. When I called him about it once, he said with good humor, "Not yet. Call back later."

Sports writers collect a lot of phone numbers. They know there is nothing more valuable than the contacts made over the course of a career. News can happen at any hour, and you want to be able to reach anyone, day or night.

The notion that a good reporter can find anyone was reinforced for me at the 1988 World Series at Dodger Stadium. Orel Hershiser was pitching for Los Angeles, and just before the start of the game the telephone rang in the auxiliary press box where I was sitting next to AP's Los Angeles sports writer, John Nadel. The sports editor wanted Nadel to find Hershiser's father, who was sitting somewhere in the ballpark, and do a piece with him talking about his son on the mound. It was a good idea but bad timing as far as Nadel was concerned, with the first pitch minutes away. Nadel hung up the phone and fulminated for 20 seconds or so about the task of finding one man among 50,000 and about how he would have to miss the game while he went off searching. Then, like the good reporter he is, he stalked off and did his job. Before the start of the second inning, Nadel was back with a broad smile. He had found Hershiser's dad, gotten some pretty good quotes, and was

ready to write. How had Nadel done it? It turned out to be simple. He asked the Dodgers' media relations representative if there was a family area in the stands for the players. The representative pointed it out to Nadel, who went down, asked around among a few people, and quickly found Orel Sr. What had seemed impossible moments earlier was accomplished with resourcefulness and effort.

Good sports writers, like all good reporters, do what they have to do and go where they have to go to get the story. That doesn't mean running over people, abusing authority, or breaking the law. It means digging hard without compromising your integrity—or the integrity of the news organization you represent. Civility and sensitivity go further than rudeness. And patience helps. Sometimes you have to wait around all day or all night or all week to get the story. Invariably, those waits, those extra efforts, pay off. Your heart beats a little stronger, your adrenaline flows a little faster, and you can't wait to call your editor and say, "Got it!" The story is yours.

Several years ago, I flew to

Marion Jones competes in the long jump finals at the U.S. Olympic Track and Field Trials in Sacramento, Calif., Sunday, July 16, 2000. (AP Photo/Doug Mills)

Tulsa, Okla., to visit with New York Jets lineman Dennis Byrd, who was recovering from temporary quadriplegia after breaking his neck in a game. I met with him at a physical rehabilitation facility and spoke with his doctors and therapists. Then, on a hunch or a hope that the devoutly religious Byrd would go to church on Sunday for the first time since the injury, I arrived early at the Assembly of God Church near his home. Halfway through the service, Byrd came in, leaning lightly on a cane and the arm of his pregnant wife. They walked slowly down the center aisle as friends and fellow worshippers applauded and wept. On that occasion, the "Got it!" feeling was overwhelmed by my own tears as I was swept up in the emotion of the scene, and the impact of both told me immediately that I had my lead.

A few years later in Camden, N.J., when former Heisman Trophy winner Mike Rozier was shot twice in the belly and once in the hand on a street corner near his home, I was as stymied as every sports writer in Philadelphia, New Jersey, and New York who tried to talk to him in the hospital or on the phone. At his instruction, the hospital wouldn't send calls or messages to him or even acknowledge that he was there, and his friends and family weren't being particularly cooperative about his condition or what led to the shooting.

I thought about Bobby Fischer and finding a way out of the jam, a way to win this journalistic game. I decided to try talking to the friend who had been shot with Rozier, Bart Merrill, whose name had been released by the police. I called the hospital, asked for Merrill and, surprisingly, was put right through. I asked if he would mind if I visited with him in his room to get his comments on the shooting. Of course, I hoped that while talking to him at his bedside, I might also find a way to see Rozier. Merrill said he didn't trust the press and was upset about the way Rozier was being portrayed in articles. I told him that I would tell his story honestly, and he agreed to talk about what happened. He asked me to come to the hospital the next day. As we sat talking in his room, Rozier shuffled in with his wounds wrapped and a drain protruding from his abdomen as he pushed around an IV pole. I introduced myself and, far from turning away or acting annoyed, he agreed to sit down for an interview in the lounge down the hall. I put a tape recorder on the table, talked with Rozier for more than an hour, then called my editor and said excitedly, "Got it!"

Many other sports writers have stories like that. Michael Wilbon of the *Washington Post* met with gang members of the Crips and Bloods at Jim Brown's house in Los Angeles after the Rodney King riots.

"I got them to reminisce about how they got into gang life," Wilbon recalls, "and they spoke about how there was a direct correlation between when their fields and parks were closed down, or could no longer be subsidized, and when they no longer had places to play. It was a departure from sports life and a transition into gang life. When I went out there, I wasn't so sure you could make this connection, but we decided to go and do it anyway. And I got gangsters talking on the record about how they went from 12-year-olds in Little League to carrying a knife."

At a Super Bowl in Los Angeles, *New York Times* columnist Dave Anderson showed his perseverance by going after former heavyweight champion Ken Norton to talk about his strained relationship with his son, Dallas Cowboys lineman Ken Norton Jr.

"I knew Ken Norton for years, back when he was a fighter," Anderson says. "I always liked him. I found out where he lived, somewhere in Newport Beach, and I drove down at night, thinking I'd just knock on his door. It turns out it's one of those gated communities, and the guy at the gate isn't going to let me in. He says, 'Norton just left.' This is about 8 o'clock. So I figure he'll

be back and I say, 'I'm just going to park my car here and when he comes back, just tell him I'm here and I'd like to talk to him.' He finally comes back 10:30 or so and I tell him I want to talk to him. He remembered me and we went up to his house and he told me his side of the story. Then I got the son's story at the regular Super Bowl sit-around-the-table press conference. Ken Norton Jr. didn't want to talk about it much, and that was fine. I had plenty from his father.

"Every now and then you've got to go after it. You can't expect it to all come to you. It's more fun, really."

Much of basic research and legwork is simply what I call "filling your notebook," keeping your eyes and ears open and writing down everything. Perhaps because I can barely read my own sloppy scrawl, I tend to write large on yellow legal pads inside a black leather cover. Most other sports writers I know use small pads that can slip inside their pockets. AP columnist Jim Litke favors the black-and-white marbled notebooks that kids use in school, the kind with the multipli-

Swimmers dive in for the final of the men's 100-meter backstroke at the Summer Olympics, Monday, Sept. 18, 2000, at the International Aquatic Center in Sydney. Lenny Krayzelburg of the United States, center, won the gold medal and set a new Olympic record with a time of 53.72. Australia's Mathew Welsh, third from bottom, took the silver and Germany's Stev Theloke, second from bottom, won the bronze. (AP Photo/Thomas Kienzle)

cation table on the back cover. Whatever's most comfortable, the idea is to jot down any detail or phrase that might enhance a story, whether it's a gamer, a column, or a feature.

During the summer of 1998, when Mark McGwire, Sammy Sosa, and Ken Griffey Jr. were mounting an assault on Roger Maris's home run record, I was just filling my notebook when I wrote down the things I saw in McGwire's open locker as I waited with a dozen other writers for him to emerge from the shower. There was a Roger Maris Celebrity Golf Tournament cap. A photo of McGwire's son, Matt, the Cardinals' batboy. A can of spinach with Popeye on the label. Sugarless chewing gum. Creatine. And a small brown bottle labeled Androstenedione.

Andro—an over-the-counter supplement that boosts testosterone levels and is banned by the Olympics, NCAA, NFL, and several other sports but not baseball—turned into the story within the story of McGwire's 70-homer year. It wasn't one I had chased or even considered but one that appeared right in front of my eyes because of a longtime habit of filling my notebook.

All the good reporters and editors I've known over the years have had a curiosity about words and facts and an obsession about accuracy. They can't stand uncertainty. Ask a tough question in any newsroom and somebody will quickly look it up. They won't just tell you to look it up; they will grab exactly the right book to check themselves because now they want to know, too. Nobody guesses in this business, not in print, anyway.

Reporters want to know everything and be sure they have it right. They live by the maxim: When in doubt, look it up. Or, if that doesn't work and the deadline is looming: When in doubt, leave it out.

A similar rule is: Never assume. Confirm everything. Be a skeptic. It's all right to ask questions. It's actually part of the job. Ask a lot of questions, the dumber the better. And listen to the answers. Litke grew up in Chicago reading Mike Royko and recalls the way he dug up stories by casting a cynical eye on things others took for granted.

"He was wonderfully skeptical," Litke says. "He had a certain innocence, though. As hard-boiled as Royko was, he would be middle of the road now. He wouldn't be considered an attack dog columnist or a Rottweiler like a lot of guys are now. There was a famous saying at the city news bureau where Royko worked: 'If your mother tells you she loves you, check it out.' So Royko would look at a deal in the city, or some parks commissioner doing something, and he'd always wonder if there is anything more to it. And a lot of times that would be

Naoko Takahashi of Japan wins the women's marathon final with a new Olympic record time of 2:23:14 at the Summer Olympics, Sunday, Sept. 24, 2000, at Olympic Stadium in Sydney. (AP Photo/Laura Rauch)

the wonderful story. There's less of that now."

Sports writers deal with tons of stats, records, and obscure factoids. Most stories don't need all those numbers, but they collect there anyway, like clods of dust, cluttering up ideas and images. The worst offense a sports writer can make is to get the numbers wrong, especially the score of a game. A close second is to spell names wrong.

"At Northwestern, you got an 'F' if you misspelled a name," recalls Christine Brennan, a Northwestern journalism school alumnus. "I am absolutely sick when I see stuff that's wrong in columns or stories. I am just nuts about accuracy. There are times when I'll go back online or read the printout of a column five times after I've sent it, and I'll call in a change or two or I'll ask an editor to read it again for me and tell me what they think. I'll double-check the spelling of names several more times. I'll take a printout with me even if I'm going out socially to dinner, so that when I call the office I can just look one more time and reassure myself that I

spelled Howard Schnellenberger correctly."

Many sports writers are inveterate collectors, filling a room or two at home with file cabinets—their own clippings, notebooks, tapes, programs, background material, articles by other writers. George Vecsey is a self-confessed "compulsive clipper" with a dozen file drawers at home, but he's found he no longer has to lug so much material with him since he can call it up on his laptop via the Internet and store it for a trip to the U.S. Open or World Series. He checks the AP each day online and does his research for events using Nexis and the *Times*'s electronic library.

"I'd be lost without being able to research and make points by finding out what we wrote about something," Vecsey says. "If I want to see what other people are writing about the U.S. Figure Skating Championships this week, and I won't be getting up there until Friday for the finals, I'll search all the papers throughout the country. I'll download what Phil Hersch (of the *Chicago Tribune*) is writing and what Christine Brennan is writing. I don't have to run out and buy 20 papers."

Litke likes to carry folders packed with newspaper and magazine clippings to events, as does Art Spander of the *Oakland Tribune.* Spander can often be seen in press rooms running clips through the copy machine, and he kindly shares his collection with grateful colleagues.

"I keep monster files," Litke says. "It's necessary if your stuff is across the board on a daily basis. It's impossible otherwise. You can't go into every situation needing basic information and not know enough to shape a reasonable opinion. I rip stuff up all the time and put it in big files. Then, before I go on a trip to cover a particular event, I'll try to find specific articles on what I'm looking at in general and read it. I pretty much stay current with everything in every sport. I don't pretend to be as well-versed as a really good beat guy on his sport, but I can pretty much tell you about every sport being played in three-quarters of the world. I've never written about cricket, but I know a frightening amount about it. I've

never written about rugby, but I know a frightening amount about it. I know bike racing and soccer and boxing. I know three or four fighters in virtually every weight class. I know a ridiculous number of baseball, football, basketball, hockey, tennis, and soccer players. I probably know as much about golf as a lot of beat writers. You have to have curiosity and you need general preparation."

Nobody knows that better than Hal Bock, who has written about sports superbly for the AP since 1963, covering more World Series and Super Bowls than any other AP sports writer. He also has covered 12 Summer and Winter Olympic Games, championship fights, the Kentucky Derby, the Indy 500, Wimbledon and U.S. Open tennis, Masters and U.S. Open golf, college football bowls and the Final Four. Few writers can match Bock's combination of versatility, speed, and clever writing under pressure.

In the first month of 2001, Bock covered two NFL playoff games followed by the Super Bowl. In between, there was an

NBA game, the baseball Hall of Fame press conference with Dave Winfield and Kirby Puckett, the introduction of new general manager Terry Bradway by the New York Jets, a women's college basketball game between Rutgers and Tennessee, and a speech by NHL commissioner Gary Bettman.

Bock knows how the games are played, and he knows how to play the sports writing game. It's his attitude, as much as his skill and knowledge, that makes him a winner. This is what Bock has to say about his versatility in the press box:

> I feel comfortable and confident covering whatever needs to be covered. That's because I have an abiding interest in all sports, not just baseball or football, not just basketball or hockey.
>
> I am intrigued by the courage of boxers, fascinated by the stamina of basketball players, shaken by the contact in football. I delight in the strategies of baseball, the speed of hockey, the individualism of tennis.
>
> I guess I am a sports junkie.
>
> This has been going on for a long time, from the time my father took me to my first baseball game and explained that those people in the press box came to the ballpark every day.
>
> And got paid for it.
>
> At age 8, I thought that would be a great way to go through life. And it has been for me. This job has taken me all over the world, from Japan to Australia, from England to Spain, from Yugoslavia to Korea. I've covered mainstream sports and I've covered obscure sports. And I pride myself on being able to do it all.
>
> The only way that's possible is to be a student of the games people play. I read our wire and two or three newspapers every day. And I don't mean just a few stories. I try to follow what's going on in all sports. I want to know when Andre Agassi and Pete Sampras decide they're going to snub the Davis Cup. And I want to know when some New Jersey teen-ager scores 100 points in a high school basketball game. I view that as doing my homework, keeping myself prepared so that I can handle anything that comes up each day.
>
> And every day is different. Nothing shakes me. I think

that goes back to the first time I wrote the lead on a World Series game. The 1972 Series between Cincinnati and Oakland went seven games. Six of them were decided by one run and several of those turned in the last inning. After going through that experience, I decided there was nothing that could throw me.

I love the characters you run into in sports, grizzled old coaches who can't get the game out of their system, hotshot rookies who believe they invented the game. I remember once asking Lou Carnesecca what kept him going, coming back year after year to coach basketball.

"The ball keeps bouncing," he said.

It was a little cryptic, I guess, but I understood.

And I remember Deion Sanders punctuating his short stay with the New York Yankees by requesting a low-numbered uniform. "Something like No. 3," he said. That would be impossible, Sanders was told, because Babe Ruth wore No. 3 and it's been out of circulation for a long time. Neon Deion settled on the less pretentious No. 21.

I look for the offbeat and it's easy to find. One year at the Kentucky Derby, I wandered out to the barns in a remote corner of Churchill Downs to talk with a trainer who was running claimers instead of Derby horses. Another time, at a big fight, I sought out an anonymous undercard boxer, whose payday was a fraction of what the big guys were getting.

These are people no one else was talking to, but they had terrific stories to tell. And I'm a good listener.

I learned a long time ago that details enrich stories. I try to give the reader snapshots, describing everything I see, even the smallest things. One time I did a piece on a journeyman fighter, the opponent who was in for a paycheck. He came into the ring with tattered shoelaces, sort of a peek into the struggle he had been through to make a living as a boxer. That became the focus of my story.

Money plays a central role in sports these days. That trend began 25 years ago and it sort of snuck up on all of us.

In the fall of 1976, when $250 million was the gross national product of some nations instead of the contract for a major league shortstop, baseball was tiptoeing ever so gingerly into the strange new world of free agency. No one knew quite what to expect, but the proprietors of the sport decided to herald its arrival in a snazzy setting. So they conducted the first draft—an exercise long ago discarded—in New York's posh Plaza Hotel.

Unaccustomed to hosting this kind of event, the hotel was not equipped with enough phone lines to accommodate the press. When Reggie Jackson was the No. 1 pick, I rushed out looking for a phone. The only one I could locate was in the vestibule of the ladies powder room. In this business, you do what you have to do. I grabbed the phone and started dictating, startling some guests but getting my story to the office.

And that's really the bottom line. Get the story. Get it first. And get it right.

Bock has done that over and over, getting the story first and getting it right, while maintaining a calmness and civility that serve him well in intense situations. If a story falls through while he's approaching deadline, he switches to Plan B and writes something else. Bock always seems to have a Plan B. He was once locked in the Montreal Forum and fell back on some high school French to get a watchman to let him out a freight entrance. He staged a staredown with a large rat in the press box at Boston Garden. It ended in a standoff, with both sides deciding on a strategic retreat. He was part of a hijacking outside Three Rivers Stadium, a half-dozen stranded writers bribing a bus driver with $5 apiece to take them back to their hotel while his regular passengers partied on after a World Series game.

"Each day is unpredictable," Bock says, "And that's how I like it."

Assignments

1. Write a sports story that requires extra legwork, perhaps tracking down a retired player or coach and people who played with them.
2. Compile a file of clips on any athlete or coach that would have enough information for an obit, and make a list of phone numbers of contacts who should be called in case you had to write the obit.
3. Compare two or three stories in newspapers about the signing of a star player or a coach, or take any other big story from several papers, to see which had the most information.

Quotes and Misquotes

In the original Golden Age of Sports, when writers were chronicling the exploits of Babe Ruth, Red Grange, and Jack Dempsey, there was no rush to interview everyone after a game or a fight. Many stories contained no quotes at all, just the eloquent or earthy observations of writers like Heywood Broun, Damon Runyon, Ring Lardner, and Frank Graham. When they did use quotes, it was more like dialogue from a play. Writers talked with athletes every day—on a train, in a hotel lobby, at dinner—but rarely in the locker room, which was the province of the players.

Even in the second Golden Age of Sports, when Willie, Mickey, and the Duke roamed center field and Jackie Robinson changed the world and Rocky Marciano ruled the ring, there was still no mad dash to get a quick quote on what kind of pitch someone hit for a homer or what kind of punch caused the knockout. If Red Smith or Jimmy Cannon used quotes at all, they were part of a narrative built exquisitely on details, never slipped in to fill space.

Germany's Yvonne Buschbaum competes in the pole vault at the Summer Olympics, Monday, Sept. 25, 2000, at Olympic Stadium in Sydney. (AP Photo/Thomas Kienzle)

Quotes and Misquotes

All that changed when sports began booming anew in the 1970s and kept right on booming through today's mega-marketed Olympics, Super Bowls, NBA Playoffs, and all the other big events that fill the sports pages, cable channels, and Internet sites. Maybe it is the influence of television or maybe it is just a shift in style to fit a new golden, diamond-studded age that celebrates celebrities, but sports writers have become more and more quote-happy with less and less concern about which quotes they choose to use. Armed with microphones and notebooks, they swarm on the fields before games and in the locker rooms afterward in search of quotes. The art of the interview has devolved to a demand for sound bites.

Sports writers do indeed need to know what the athletes and coaches have to say, what they're thinking about, what they plan to do. But gathering quotes doesn't necessarily mean using them. Any good writer can write better than most people can speak. And many quotes are simply better off not being preserved for posterity. "I was very focused," "we didn't execute properly on offense," and "they played a great game" don't exactly punch up a story.

"There are too many quotes in newspapers. It's just ridiculous," the *Washington Post*'s Michael Wilbon says. "And the quotes I read in newspapers are just awful. I don't know when it started, but I'm not going to add to that. I'm looking for quotes that actually say something. It goes back to that phrase, 'I can say it better than they can,' with the notable exceptions of a Shannon Sharpe and a Charles Barkley, people who are either incredibly brilliant or funny or have their own way of using the language. I don't need the quotes; I need information so I can feel certain about a point of view that I am sending. When you're doing beat stuff you need more quotes. But even as a beat writer I didn't rely on quotes."

Wilbon uses far fewer quotes in his columns and stories than most writers, and the best writers are always judicious in the quotes they choose. AP's Jim Litke rarely uses more than two or three sentences from anyone. The *New York Times*'s Dave Anderson tends to quote people more often, feeling the athletes' words give the

The Japanese team performs their routine underwater during the Olympic synchronized swimming final competition, Friday, Sept. 29, 2000, in Sydney, Australia. The team finished in second place. (AP Photo/Robert F. Bukaty)

story a greater sense of authenticity for readers.

"I think people like to read quotes," Anderson says. "That's what made Frank Graham great. He was the greatest dialogue sports writer we've ever had. It was like eavesdropping on some good conversation. Not many subjects lend themselves to that. Muhammad Ali did. You could just get up in the morning and find Ali and follow him around and go to his workout and you had a column. He was wonderful. Just let him talk."

The subject and the story influence the approach. Sometimes a game story or even a feature can read better with fewer quotes. Sometimes it works to let the subject's voice carry the piece. Most often, it's somewhere in between. There are no rules, except those that govern good judgment and taste.

In most cases, there is no reason to quote someone on factual details or routine observations such as, "We outplayed them and beat them by 20 points," or, "It was raining pretty hard out there."

Even many feelings or opinions can be paraphrased and, probably, tightened or expressed in a better way:

"I just loved the ups and downs of the games," head coach Sara Jones said. "It was the same thing with each season. Hopefully we won more than we lost, but they both built character."

Or: She loved the rhythms of the games and the seasons, the successes and failures that gave her teams character.

When paraphrasing, though, exercise extreme caution and be absolutely faithful to the meaning and tone of the original quote. This is not the place to get too creative. The goal is clarity, not distortion. If there is even the slightest concern that the paraphrase does not reflect exactly what was said, stick with the quote or avoid the reference altogether.

In general, save quotation marks for the unique and colorful lines that jump out from the prose around them, express the voice and views of the subject, or help to evoke the scene, such as this one when the U.S. women's softball team won at the Sydney Olympics:

"Come on, bring it on, rain," a thoroughly soaked Michele Smith shouted, tossing her head back to feel the rain splash on her face as she opened her arms and twirled in delight. "This has been our whole experience. Rain and hard luck. Tough, tough games. And now, finally, gold."

It's almost always easier to talk to winners after games. They're in a good mood and are more likely to banter with writers and teammates. They linger in the locker room a little longer, enjoying the moment. Many players, especially in baseball, prefer not to talk too much about themselves. But ask them about a teammate's contribution to the victory and they'll wax poetic—or at least as poetic as they can get.

Losing locker rooms, from high schools to the pros, take on the mournful solemnity of a funeral parlor. Voices are lowered, heads are bowed, and no one dares smile. Writers tend to enter cautiously and respectfully, as if they were intruders at a private service. Yet in that moment, when everyone is a bit on edge, ballplayers may utter some of their most cogent and insightful lines. A losing locker room, especially after a

Denver Broncos quarterback John Elway celebrates a fourth-quarter touchdown against the Atlanta Falcons in Super Bowl XXXIII in Miami, Sunday, Jan. 31, 1999. (AP Photo/Doug Mills)

big game, is never easy, but it is always worth the trip.

Some of the best places to talk to people are in their homes, their offices, their cars, or, if you can work it out, on airplanes, where they can't walk out the door for three or four hours. One of my favorite interviews came with Barry Bonds just after he had been slammed in a cover story in *Sports Illustrated* by a reporter who had

trouble getting an interview with him. Bonds came across in the SI piece as distant, egocentric, and uncooperative, which was not the way he seemed to most of the Giants beat writers I had spoken to about him. They got along with him fine, though he had his days. When I approached Bonds for a feature story, he said he couldn't talk at length before a game because his mind was on what he had to do on the field. Then he didn't want to talk after a game because he was exhausted. That went on for two or three days. I said, fine, how about if we talk on an off-day, maybe on the flight to Chicago in a few days for the Giants' series with the Cubs? He agreed, so I arranged it with the Giants' front office and we talked for most of the flight from San Francisco, with me tape-recording it all the way. Bonds showed up that day wearing a silky banana-yellow shirt, and he came across as friendly and thoughtful. It got to the point where I wasn't even asking him a lot of questions. He was just telling stories and joking around, totally relaxed, and he kept talking buoyantly to his teammates on the bus from the airport to the downtown hotel. It was a side of Bonds that I hadn't seen and that hadn't been written about, and it added another dimension to my understanding of him.

I've always felt that the most effective way to interview people is to try to understand what's going on inside their mind and their life, to empathize with them and ask questions that will draw out what they think. That doesn't mean always agreeing with them or acting phony, but approaching them with sensitivity and challenging them when it's appropriate. Some writers, like the *Los Angeles Times*'s T.J. Simers, tend to be more confrontational, putting their subjects on edge, and that works for them. Everyone has his or her own style:

George Vecsey: "You don't need to interrogate or be a wise guy or play around with them. The sooner you can get people to calm down and talk, the more likely you are to have a real conversation. The idea of a journalist is to get small, to stoop down psychologically and listen. Let them know you're interested in what they say. The sooner you shut up and listen to them, the better. It sounds manipulative, but, in fact, when people are talking they often say interesting things. Then you can casually say, 'Well, I don't understand that. Could you get into that a little more?' But just get people to talk. Don't think you have to ask a million questions."

Christine Brennan: "Kindness and friendliness help. Not being in their face. Even if it's going to end up being an in-your-face kind of story, there's nothing wrong with being kind and fair to people. Sometimes you can put them on their heels. If it's someone who wants to come fight right back, there will be great stuff from them. It depends on knowing your subject, doing your homework, working harder than anybody else ahead of time so you're prepared for it.

"It's better to interview someone in person than on the phone, but many times you must do it on the phone. Try to find a good time for them.

"There's the old line about saving the tough questions for last so that if they walk away or hang up, at least you have something. On the other hand, you don't want them to stop before you even get to the tough stuff.

"There are times when I will write down the questions and have them in front of me during the interview. Other times, I don't. If there's any doubt, there's nothing wrong with writing down your questions or notes to yourself about things to ask so that you're prepared."

Dave Anderson: "Just ask them the questions that you think the reader wants to get the answer to. You're the reader's man. I've always thought that we are real privileged in that we can go to locker rooms and talk to players and managers and coaches. That's what a reader would love to be able to do."

Ira Berkow: "There's no need to be confrontational, but never be a pussycat or a pushover. If you don't agree with somebody, your place to disagree is in print, unless it's helpful in the interview to have a discussion or play devil's advocate.

"You're trying to be sensitive to them to find out what they're thinking. Willie Mays once taught me a very important lesson. He had just hit his 600th home run and it was near the end of his career. So I said, 'Willie, how much longer do you think you can play?' In his very high-pitched voice, he says, 'How come everyone is always asking me, "Willie, how much longer you gonna play?" Do they want me to leave baseball? I just hit my 600th home run. How come people don't say, "Willie, congratulations on 600 home runs." ' I said, 'Willie, you're

Baltimore Ravens head coach Brian Billick hoists the Vince Lombardi trophy aloft after the Ravens' 34-7 defeat of the New York Giants at Raymond James Stadium during Super Bowl XXXV in Tampa, Fla., Sunday, Jan. 28, 2001. Ravens owner Art Modell is second from left. (AP Photo/Elise Amendola)

absolutely right. It was a fantastic achievement. Congratulations on hitting 600 home runs.' I asked him one or two other questions, and then I said, 'You ever get tired of playing baseball?' You know, coming at it in another way to get where I wanted to be.

"These are all great achievers, all these people that I'm interviewing, for the most part. There's always a way to say something positive to begin a conversation that's not false or subservient. Saying congratulations for something that's legitimate never hurts. Even Willie Mays had to be told congratulations on 600 home runs. Sometimes I forget it at my peril. It's helpful to have a sense of who they are as fallible human beings and not just as sports stars."

The interview room, despite its name, is probably the worst place in sports to interview anyone. It is a concept that thwarts spontaneity and usually produces the most vapid quotes. Nobody is comfortable. Not the writers, looking up like schoolchildren with notebooks, raising their hands to a team or league flack to ask a question as a microphone is passed around the room. Not the athletes, sitting at a table raised up on a platform, squinting out through blinding TV lights, unable to tell who or where the questions are coming from.

The interview room is one of the necessary evils of modern sport—there are many others, such as agents and shoe reps—and it evolved out of the simple fact that there are too many people covering games who need quotes quickly. Where once, back in the 1970s, there might have been a dozen writers at the NBA Playoffs or the U.S. Open Tennis Championships, now there are a couple hundred media types of all stripes, sticking mikes and lights in players' faces, looking for quotes.

With some players, the interview room is the only place to catch them before they're out the door. They retreat to the trainer's room or block out everyone with headsets until they deign to give the press a 10-minute audience. "I don't talk before the game," Reggie Miller would say politely but firmly. "I do the interview room after the game, then I'm gone." Patrick Ewing also didn't talk on the record before games. Mike Wilbon talked to him anyway for about 15 minutes each game he covered. Wilbon never took out his notebook, just chatted with him casually and found out everything he wanted to know, though not for quotation.

At big events, it's become customary to provide verbatim transcripts of the interviews, a service that is helpful for writers but also laden with peril for them. The quote sheets are quick and quite accurate. They allow writers to avoid the interview room, knowing they can always pick up the quote sheets later. But there are dangers in merely reading the quotes without attending the interview. Sometimes meaning is conveyed by a facial expression, a gesture, or the tone of what was said. Irony or sarcasm can be lost. A missing comma can change an innocent comment into a serious mistake. The interview room may yield few memorable quotes, but most writers go there anyway, just covering the bases and doing the job. Staying away can leave questions unasked and unanswered.

Some writers, who may be covering an event alone or with very few colleagues, skip the interview room and don't bother with the quote sheets, preferring to rely on what they can gather in the clubhouse. Others go to both. A few just wait for the transcripts. At the U.S. Open, it's not unusual for writers, especially those on deadline, to watch the interviews on closed-circuit TV at their workstations in the windowless press box under the stadium.

There are all kinds of interviews in all kinds of places, and there isn't always time to find out everything you want to know. When possible, it's often helpful to ease tension and encourage thought by interviewing people at a slow, conversational pace. Let the situation, whether serious or light, guide your demeanor. Resist playing the psychologist, the critic, the comic, the moralist, the know-it-all, or the judge.

Ask open-ended questions that don't limit or manipulate answers as do closed-ended questions, which often produce evasive or one-word responses. Rather than asking, "Do you think you can win the Super Bowl?" and getting an answer like, "Yeah, sure," try, "Talk about the biggest factors for you to win the Super Bowl." And follow it up with other sides of the issue: "What worries you about the other team? Talk about the biggest challenges you face individually and as a team." People are often ambivalent about things, and it's important to draw out their doubts and misgivings. By approaching issues from two or three sides, asking about the good and the bad in situations, you gain a deeper understanding.

Avoid prejudging people, thinking you know what they will say or how they will act because of things you've heard about them. People will often surprise you and give you something new.

Consider what someone has gone through in life, not to psychoanalyze but to appreciate it and understand them a little better.

Most important of all, listen intently and purposefully. Don't miss what someone is saying by letting your mind wander or your eyes drift around the room, or by rehearsing the next question. Pay attention and stay neutral, neither judging the people you're interviewing nor encouraging them to judge you. Establish eye contact and a posture that shows you are listening. Empathize by projecting yourself into their shoes; don't always sympathize by pouring out the emotions you may share. Listen for unique phrasing, tone, and viewpoint. Watch gestures, posture and facial expressions. A wince, a shrug, a sly smile can be more meaningful than words.

Turn an interview into a conversation by thinking on your feet and veering away at times from prepared questions to ask good follow-ups that flow naturally from a gesture or something that is said. Pursue ideas and introspection rather than just sound bites, but listen closely for the quotes that will light up a story. Keep talking and probing until

you get those quotes. Restate what they say to make sure you understand, and listen to their whole story.

Become an effective listener by being a reflective listener, taking what they are saying and reflecting it back to clarify feelings and meanings so that they know you are listening. Reflective listening provides sort of a mirror for them to see themselves more clearly and often elicits a response that sharpens a reporter's own understanding of what they mean or how they feel.

COACH: We will never win games if we keep making mistakes like that.

REPORTER: You sound angry and disappointed. What are you going to do about it?

Avoid a closed response, which indicates that you have neither heard nor understood what was said. Closed responses tend to cut off communication. In contrast, an open response indicates that you have heard and understood, and it reflects what was said in a way that shows you also have picked up the feelings behind the words.

ATHLETE: My leg hasn't healed as fast as I thought it would, but there's nothing I can do about it.

CLOSED RESPONSE: That's life.

OPEN RESPONSE: You're feeling helpless, aren't you?

The first response doesn't accept the athlete's feelings and suggests that they don't matter. It shuts down communication. The second response recognizes his or her feelings, shows acceptance and concern, and encourages the athlete to tell you more.

Some sports writers use a tape or digital recorder for every interview, some only for a feature when there is time to transcribe quotes. Others rely solely on notes. Even if you use a recorder, it's a good idea to take notes as a backup to a malfunctioning machine, dead batteries, or some other mishap. That's a lesson I learned in my first taped interview when I slyly, and foolishly, placed the recorder on the chair between me and New York Knicks center Willis Reed at a restaurant. When I played back the tape, all I heard were muffled voices and the clatter of silverware. I hadn't been concentrating on taking notes, but fortunately I had written enough and remembered enough of what he said so that the inaudible tape didn't matter. In general, I avoid interviews over meals because of the awkwardness in taking notes.

Recorders can come in handy in packed locker rooms, where you have to wedge in and reach over or through a mass of writers to get anything. Recorders virtually guarantee accuracy and are helpful in picking up the nuances of people's speech and the subtle things they say that could be missed by just taking notes. Recordings also allow you to refresh your mind about everything in the interview before starting a story.

The main drawback to tape recording interviews is speed and convenience. It often takes three or four times as long to transcribe a tape as it does to conduct the interview, even with the use of a transcription machine equipped with a foot pedal. Even if you are transcribing only highlights, it can take a long time to go through it all. I have spent a large chunk of my career transcribing interviews, mostly for features and investigative series, and it is the most tedious, time-consuming part of

Tennessee Titans wide receiver Kevin Dyson (87) is tackled short of the goal line by St. Louis Rams linebacker Mike Jones on the final play of Super Bowl XXXIV to preserve the Rams 23-16 win on Sunday, Jan. 30, 2000, in Atlanta. (AP Photo/Michael Conroy)

the job. I've done it because I feel listening to the tapes, typing out the quotes, and reading the transcripts refreshes my memory (especially when I'm interviewing many people for a story), brings out small details that I might have missed, and gives me an accurate take on what people are saying and how they're saying it. Using a tape recorder also allows me to pay more attention to an athlete's looks and gestures during the interview. A transcript can be like a trellis of words on which to hang a story, even if most of the quotes fade away in the telling.

Someday—probably the day I retire—somebody will invent a recording device advanced enough to distinguish different voices and meaning accurately with a college band playing in the background and will equip it with a digital disk or computer link so that perfect transcripts can be printed out immediately. Unfortunately, affordable voice recognition systems haven't come that far yet. When they do, reporters will be among the first to grab them.

For beat writers covering a game, there's usually no time to listen to tapes and transcribe everything, though a tape can provide a good backup to notes if it's necessary to review a quote. Columnists tend not to use tape recorders, in part because of deadline pressure and in part because they use fewer quotes as they emphasize color and commentary.

George Vecsey: "I write down the key things and sometimes I'm surprised how good I am in getting the essence of it. Once in a

while I am surprised that there were things I missed. People are telling me things that are important to them. If I know, generally, what it is I'm working with that day, I don't need every word that the person is saying. I sure need his answers to things and specifics, but I'm comfortable enough with note taking.

"I have done about 10 books. I always use a tape recorder for them because I want to hear speech patterns.

"I have notepads for 25 years in order, with the themes and dates on the outside. The reason goes back to when I was a news reporter. I wrote a story and about a year later some lawyer called me, saying somebody was claiming that I made stuff up about a coal mine disaster. I said, 'Let me tell you something, it's all in my notebook in the same color ink.' I went back and found the notepad. That taught me a lesson, so I have never thrown my notebooks away. I go in order in the notebooks and write line by line. I could put my hand on 80 to 90 percent [of the interviews] I have done in the last 25 years. I don't go back that often, though. It's just there. The day I retire, nobody's going to want it and I'll throw them out."

Michael Wilbon: "I take notes and hardly ever tape record. The key is to listen. Some people are so busy getting quotes, they're not listening. There's no conversation going on. People should listen more for information and not just the sound bite. We are all into sound bite mode now."

Ira Berkow: "I take notes and probably 90 percent of what I write down I don't use. You can take voluminous notes, but then when you sit down to write the story you don't have to look at the notes at all because you're immersed in the story. So I write a 2,000- or 3,000-word story without looking at my notes. I mean, I know the whole story. I've lived this story. And I write the whole story down. At one point I write, 'The man said to his wife, "Jump off the roof." ' OK, now I go back to my notes and I see exactly what he had said to his wife, 'Look, honey, you're going to have to jump off the roof in two minutes,' or something like that. So I can go back to get the line exactly, but I do that only after

I've written the story so that the whole flow is there first.

"A lot of times guys tape people and, since they know they're getting it, their mind sort of drifts. I am giving total attention, so I'm getting the way the ballplayer looks, the way he shrugs. I've seen guys tape people in interviews in locker rooms, and they're sort of looking away. They have the tape extended with other people around and they're dreaming about something else. Well, here I'm watching this guy, watching his movements, listening to what he says and responding to him. I see a lot of people sometimes don't even respond to some of the things that are said.

"I learned from Red Smith that you just listen closely to particular phrases. When you get them, you can quote almost verbatim. I've done that on a number of occasions.

"There are times when I feel I can't take out my notebook. I'll go along talking without a notebook, and maybe after 15 minutes or so I'll say, 'You just told me an address. I better write it down because I'm not going to remember this address.' I take out my notebook and write down the address. And then we talk some more. Now I start taking notes because they feel comfortable. And if there was something that they had said in the first 15 minutes that I wanted and I didn't 100 percent remember, I'll go back, and they'll go into telling me the story again. They'll repeat themselves.

"Some people do feel more comfortable when they see you taking notes or using a tape recorder because they feel you'll be more accurate. Once I interviewed Marianne Moore, the poet. I wasn't taking notes. She said, 'I feel more comfortable if you take notes.' She got a couple of pieces of paper and a pencil for me. I had my pad and pen, but she went and got them for me, so I started taking notes with her paper and pencil because she felt more comfortable."

Christine Brennan: "After you've done the interview, if you're not certain about something, call them back, if possible. There have been quite a few times when I've called someone. If it's a real sensitive issue, antagonistic or something, or if I have any doubts, I'll call them back and say, 'I just want to check this quote.' I'm not getting an OK from them on this. The quote is the quote. But I want to read it back to them. Kind of like doing my own fact checking. There's nothing wrong with that. You're not letting them change the quote. You're not letting them edit the piece. You're just reading the quote back. I don't do this as a normal practice, but every now and then. It's my story; it's their life. I try to keep that in my mind the whole time."

Though some athletes, coaches, and others won't talk about their private lives, many others will. They are not obligated to divulge their darkest secrets and innermost thoughts—that's not part of the reader's right to know—but that doesn't prevent reporters from asking when it's appropriate and pertinent. Probing personal questions can trigger silence, anger, or a flood of fascinating quotes. In the case of Jennifer Capriati at the U.S. Open a few years ago, the questions triggered tears. The key is to be sensitive and to try to approach personal issues in private. That's not always possible. At the Open, Capriati, like nearly all the players, was available only in the interview room.

Sports writers and athletes share a symbiotic relationship. They need each other, feed off each other. Reporters serve as a link between athletes and fans, who buy the newspapers and the tickets to games. It is a relationship that used to be understood implicitly in sports in the days when athletes weren't so fantastically rich. These days, an awful lot of athletes see the press as an annoyance or even a threat. They concede to interviews reluctantly, reveal their disdain with shrugs or sarcastic cracks, then dash off in their limos. Jim Courier acted that way for years. Then when he retired and took a job as a television commentator, he had a sudden insight. He realized that athletes need the press and have an obligation to their fans through the press. Courier said he wished someone had explained that to him when he was younger.

Sports writers should expect, even demand, cooperation, if not cordiality, from athletes and coaches. Access through open locker rooms and interviews is essential. The associations that represent writers covering each of the major sports—the Baseball Writers Association of America, the International Tennis Writers Association, and so on—exist in large part to ensure continued access for reporters. Some athletes and coaches may loathe us, but the teams and leagues and tour officials issue press credentials because they want us to cover their events.

That doesn't mean sports writers should expect athletes and coaches to perform for them.

"Some writers tend to denigrate people who aren't wonderful quotes," Dave Anderson says. "They think a guy is a bad person if he doesn't act like a standup comic. Some of our subjects are very shy people who just don't have a lot to say. If a guy is always very quiet and introspective, then, hey, he doesn't have to change for me. If he doesn't tell me a lot, that's my problem, not his problem."

Pete Sampras is one of those quiet guys who rarely says anything memorable. He may be one of the greatest tennis players in history, but he doesn't come close to sparkling in interviews the way Andre Agassi, John McEnroe, and Jimmy Connors do. Many writers have condemned Sampras for being dull, but he can no more come up with brilliantly witty one-liners than McEnroe could control his temper. Sampras has made no secret of his distaste for the press in general and the interview process in particular. Of all the interview rooms at the Grand Slam tournaments, Sampras seems most comfortable at Wimbledon, where All-England Club officials stare at their watches as they sit beside the players and do their best to keep interviews brief and innocuous.

Situations like that stand in sharp contrast to the cooperation given by other sports stars, especially older ones who understand the relationship to the press. Some of my favorite interviews have been with athletes in their 70s, 80s, and 90s.

While working on a series on Hall of Fame ballplayers several years ago, I called up Bobby Doerr, the Boston Red Sox second baseman in the 1930s and 1940s and a longtime teammate of Ted Williams. When I asked Doerr if I could visit with him on his ranch in Eugene, Oregon, he said, sure, so we set a date. Then I asked for directions so I could drive a rental car out from the airport. Doerr told me not to bother, just let him know when I was arriving and he and his wife would pick me up at the airport and drive me back afterward. I was astonished. At a time when rude and/or inaccessible athletes had become common, the 76-year-old Doerr was a refreshing throwback to an era when civility was more customary.

As it turned out, I spent six hours with Doerr at his home, had lunch with him and his wife, Monica, and thoroughly enjoyed listening to his stories as he flipped through his scrapbooks and showed off his baseball memorabilia. At one point, Doerr gently lifted Babe Ruth's signed bat off the brass hook in the myrtle wood case where it resided, as if on an altar, beside the bats of Ted Williams and Ty Cobb and Joe DiMaggio.

"You feel that, you've felt something Ruth had," Doerr said with a tone of pride and reverence.

Doerr's words carried the story right down to the end when he said: "I look around this room and there are so many memories. We had so much fun. It's getting to the point now where time is running out for a lot of us. We're getting closer to the end of the bench."

Locker Room Talk

The record for the most obscenities in an interview probably belongs to former Los Angeles Dodgers manager Tommy Lasorda, who once spewed out something like 142 curse words in a 5-minute discourse before a game. He wasn't angry at anything. He was just being typically Tommy—funny and serious, loud and bombastic, enjoying himself and his audience of sports writers. Copies of a tape recording of that foul-mouthed monologue made the rounds in baseball and became a minor classic among writers.

Lasorda could hardly talk to beat writers without throwing in dozens of obscenities as adjectives, verbs, adverbs, and every other part of speech. Yet amazingly, the moment he was being interviewed for radio or television, Lasorda switched to a censored mode and never said a single word that would have gotten him in trouble with his mother.

The problem with trying to quote ballplayers and coaches accurately is that sometimes a fair chunk of what they say can't be printed in family newspapers or on the AP wire. What readers sometimes get is a sanitized version of sports speak that doesn't sound anything like the more realistic dialogue heard in movies such as *Any Given Sunday* with Al Pacino.

Either we don't quote the scurrilous speech of players or we paraphrase them or we clean up their quotes, in part because a slew of vulgarities is offensive to many readers and in part because they are usually gratuitous, meaningless words that are tossed around as commonly as "like" and "y'know." Instead of adding color to a ballplayer's speech, they get in the way of what he's trying to say. They may be part of the quote, but there is no compelling reason to use them.

Good judgment is required in knowing where to draw the line, but the guiding principle is to be faithful to the quote and never change its meaning or context.

To quote some athletes accurately—and strictly according to the *Associated Press Stylebook* rules—would mean filling nearly every routine sports story with hyphens and ellipses and making them virtually impossible to read: "We would have . . . won the . . . game if the . . . ref had made the . . . call before the . . . clock . . . ran out." In taking notes, sports writers usually just use common sense in filtering out those profanities and simplifying the sentence: "We would have won the game if the ref had made the call before the clock ran out."

In general, though, sports writers should adhere to the same *AP Stylebook* rules that govern the use of quotations and obscenities in all news stories:

Quotations in the news Never alter quotations even to correct minor grammatical errors or word usage. Casual minor tongue slips may be removed by using ellipses but even that should be done with extreme caution. If there is a question about a quote, either don't use it or ask the speaker to clarify.

Do not routinely use abnormal spellings such as *gonna* in attempts to convey regional dialects or mispronunciations. Such spellings are appropriate when relevant or help to convey a desired touch in a feature.

FULL vs. PARTIAL QUOTES: In general, avoid fragmentary quotes. If a speaker's words are clear and concise, favor the full quote. If cumbersome language can be paraphrased fairly, use an indirect construction,

reserving quotation marks for sensitive or controversial passages that must be identified specifically as coming from the speaker.

CONTEXT: Remember that you can misquote someone by giving a startling remark without its modifying passage or qualifiers. The manner of delivery sometimes is part of the context. Reporting a smile or a deprecatory gesture may be as important as conveying the words themselves.

Obscenities, profanities, vulgarities Do not use them in stories unless they are part of direct quotations and there is a compelling reason for them. When a profanity, obscenity or vulgarity is used, flag the story at the top:

Editors: Language in 4th graf may be offensive to some readers.

Then confine the offending language, in quotation marks, to a separate paragraph that can be deleted easily by editors who do not want it.

In reporting profanity that normally would use the words *damn* or *god*, lowercase *god* and use the following forms: *damn, damn it, goddamn it.* Do not, however, change the offending words to euphemisms. Do not, for example, change *damn it* to *darn it.*

If a full quote that contains profanity, obscenity, or vulgarity cannot be dropped but there is no compelling reason for the offensive language, replace letters of an offensive word with a hyphen. The word *damn*, for example, would become *d__* or ____.

When the subject matter of a story may be considered offensive, but the story does not contain quoted profanity, obscenities or vulgarities, flag the story at the top:

Editors: The contents may be offensive to some readers.

Anonymous Sources

Several years ago, when a bookie I interviewed for a series on illegal sports gambling asked me not to identify him because he feared getting blown away by the Mafia, I readily agreed. He had good inside information on a huge offshore betting operation and confirmed details I had heard from the FBI and other bookmakers. But I had no particular desire to put him, or myself, at risk for the sake of a scoop. We are talking sports, after all, not national security.

Aside from that instance and a handful of others, I've avoided quoting anonymous sources. If someone doesn't want to be identified, I'd rather not quote that person at all, even if it means getting beat on a story. Most of the time it hasn't come to that. I'll usually find someone else to talk on the record or persuade the reluctant source to change his or her mind.

I've generally distrusted quotes attributed to anonymous sources, whether in the news or sports sections, and feel they weaken rather than strengthen stories and tend to undermine the credibility of newspapers. Certainly anonymous sources have a place in our business, but like many other journalists and readers, I'd prefer seeing them less often.

Here are the AP's basic rules about anonymous sources:

- The material must be factual information—*not* speculation or opinion. (That goes double for any attack or defense of others under cover of anonymity.)
- The information must be *critical* to the story, not just a colorful quote or an elaboration.
- The material must be unavailable except on conditions of anonymity imposed by the source.
- The reporter must know the source to be reliable and in a position to have accurate information. The reporter needs to know how the source knows the information to be accurate.

Once these conditions are met, a story should provide as much background as possible to establish the informant's credentials and credibility. For example, "according to a Yankees official," or "according to a participant in the meeting."

Information from an unidentified source should always be a last resort.

Assignments

1. Interview two people, one by phone and one in person, using notes in one case and a tape recorder in the other. Write an 800-word story from each interview.
2. Compare three sports stories about the same subject that used quotes extensively. Did the quotes match? How did each writer handle the use of quotes? Which was most effective, and why?
3. Interview five classmates, friends, or family members for 10 minutes each, taking notes and using a tape recorder. Transcribe the recorded interviews and compare them for accuracy with written notes.

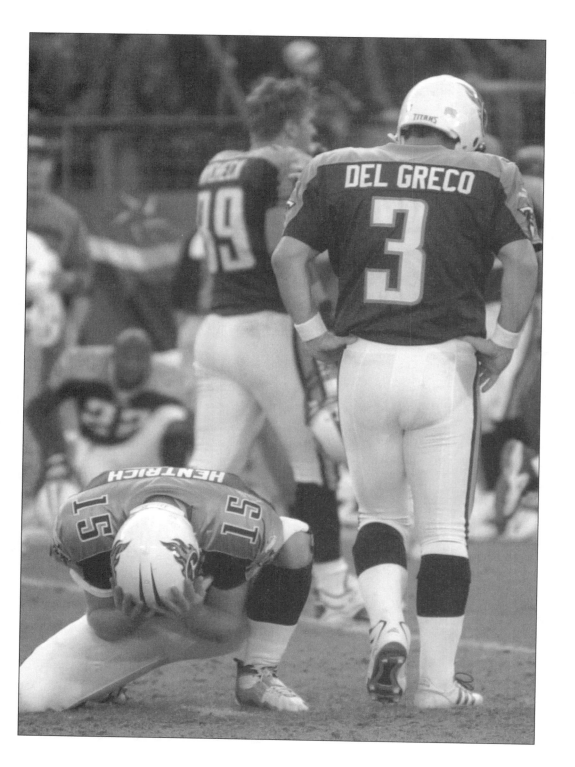

Beyond the Fields:
Features, Enterprise, and Investigative Reporting

From my first days as a sports writer, working nights and wandering into half-empty movie theaters on gray afternoons in New York, my feature stories have been influenced by films: images, dialogue, the unfolding of the narrative chronologically or with flashbacks, spanning generations in two hours, condensing lifetimes into moments. I've aimed for stories with a sense of visual movement and the sound of a character's voice. Stories rich with mood and drama that could go with buttered popcorn as much as with morning coffee.

Feature writers have the luxury of escaping the daily deadlines and the boundaries of game coverage, and they leave opinions and essays to the columnists. Though there are no rules, features are often more like nonfiction short stories—narratives that never play loose with facts and quotes, yet use the techniques of fiction.

Even at great length, well-written features don't read long.

Tennessee Titans place kicker Al Del Greco (3) walks off the field as holder Craig Hentrich (15) shows his dejection after Del Greco missed a 43-yard field goal as time ran out against the Baltimore Ravens on Sunday, Nov. 12, 2000, in Nashville, Tenn. Baltimore defeated Tennessee 24-23. Behind Hentrich is tight end Frank Wycheck (89). (AP Photo/John Russell)

There's no fat, no florid, sentimental prose. They use lean, emphatic language to achieve sharp, true images—simple nouns and verbs delivering clean, swift motions. Metaphors are precise, fitting, original, not forced. They are stories built on an accumulation of details, facts, quotes, thoughts, sights, sounds, scents, touch, and taste. They cleave always to the truth of the place, the characters, the story. There is a difference between writing abstractly about a ballplayer with AIDS and sitting at his bedside, observing him closely, as I did with Glenn Burke:

> He had the whispered voice of a dying man, purple Kaposi's sarcoma lesions on grotesquely swollen feet burning into his body "worse than a sharp pain . . . it's a killing pain." He stared at his sores, then turned to the ceiling, squeezing his eyes shut, grinding his chipped teeth together, clenching his fists. . . . Burke looked so scrawny and weak in a T-shirt, boxer shorts and socks. He lay curled on the bed without a blanket, autumn sunlight slanting through a window in the hot room. . . . His feet were lumpy and useless, riddled with tumors, and he had to drag himself on aluminum crutches to get out of bed. His weight was down from 220 as a player to 145. Soon he would begin radiation treatment, soon he would need a walker, soon a wheelchair, soon . . ."

When *Sports Illustrated*'s Leigh Montville wrote about the Zambian national soccer team that had perished in a plane crash, he brought readers with him as he stood "in the middle of the arid African landscape on a warm afternoon, surrounded by the thirty mounds of earth, not knowing where to look first. The dust blows into your face. The sun beats onto your head. You try to catalog all of the feelings, try to capture the sight and the emotions in words, but how can you do that? You stand and mostly you gape. . . . You look at all the pictures, one picture behind each of the thirty mounds. Many of the black faces are so young, faces that could be from a yearbook, from a college football program on a Saturday afternoon. . . . The dust and the sun have turned the edges of the pictures a faded

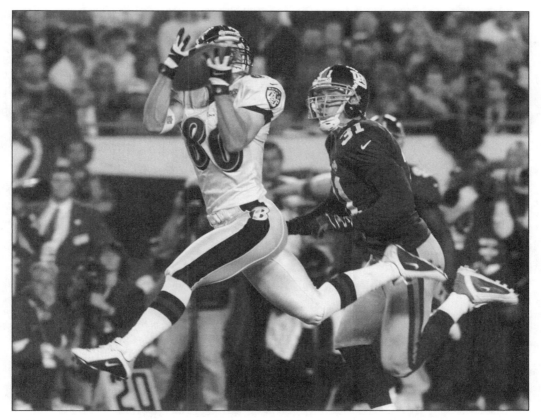

Baltimore Ravens' wide receiver Brandon Stokley (80) hauls in a 38-yard touchdown pass in front of New York Giants' cornerback Jason Sehorn in the first quarter of Super Bowl XXXV on Sunday, Jan. 28, 2001, in Tampa, Fla. (AP Photo/Doug Mills)

brown in five months' time. Everything seems faded. The remnants of burial wreaths cover each of the graves, the colors of the satin ribbons faded, the real flowers long gone, the artificial flowers also faded. Plastic sheets have been laid over some of the graves, helping to keep the presentations intact. Cinder blocks have been set upon the sheets to keep them in place. The cinder blocks are chipped and brown, the plastic colored brown, again from the dust. Everything is brown."

So much reporting goes into good feature writing that the actual writing of the story, as

A slow-shutter exposure captures the camera flashes from all around Busch Stadium as they attempt to record history during the first pitch of the first at-bat of St. Louis Cardinals home run slugger Mark McGwire against the Chicago Cubs, in St. Louis, Tuesday, Sept. 8, 1998. McGwire tied with Roger Maris for most home runs in a single season with 61. McGwire grounded out on the play. (AP Photo/Ed Reinke)

thoughtful and graceful as it may be, often is the least time-consuming part. Reporters may go around for days or weeks filling notebooks with details, quotes, facts. They may have several 90-minute tapes filled with interviews, carry around a file bulging with dozens of clips and photocopied documents. They may read a book or two or three for background. But when they are done researching and have spread all that material out around them and absorbed as much of it as possible, they can bring it all together in a feature in a day.

Even in event coverage, most notes never get into a story. At a tennis match, diligent reporters keep notes on every point and jot down thoughts along the way. Yet probably 90 percent of that gets tossed in the end while they focus

A young Baltimore Orioles fan is overcome with emotion after asking Oriole Cal Ripken Jr. for his autograph after the Orioles game with the New York Yankees on Sunday, Oct. 1, 2000, at Camden Yards in Baltimore. The Orioles beat the Yankees 7-3. Ripken threw out balls to the fans and signed autographs after the Orioles swept the Yankees 3 games to 0. (AP Photo/Dave Hammond)

Lightning flashes around Turner Field in Atlanta during a rain delay in the Braves' game with the St. Louis Cardinals, Thursday, Aug. 24, 2000. (AP Photo/John Bazemore)

on a few key points, the overall tenor of the match, the significance of the outcome, and other issues. They just never know until the match is over which 10 percent will be relevant to the story. The same is true with a running at a basketball game or a box score and notes at a baseball game. It all helps to keep track of what's going on and to have a record to look back on, but only a small percentage survives in a story.

That happens, in a much more magnified way, when researching a feature.

Ira Berkow sees similarities with the research that goes into many novels—the accumulation of details that authors sift through to produce exquisitely descriptive scenes:

Philip Roth is one of our great novelists and in his recent book *American Pastoral* the main character was in the glove manufacturing business. The detail of glove manufacturing is fantastic. It reminded me of the detail in *Moby Dick* about whaling. I mean you are on that ship in *Moby Dick,* you're rocking with the waves. In *American Pastoral* you could smell the leather in the leather factory.

"You go out and you spend a lot of time talking to people. You really can't get enough information. It's like the famous Hemingway line that a piece of writing is only one-eighth of the iceberg and the other seven-eighths is research that doesn't get used. The writer omits many of the things that he knows but the reader still gets a strong feeling of those things. If you write, you will understand it. If you don't write, you probably won't understand it. But the more information you have, the more knowledgeable the writer is, the more selective you can be in the details that move a story.

When Berkow sits down to write after all his research is complete—or as complete as time and circumstances allow—he goes through his notebook to refresh himself on the details of the story, then he sets the notebook aside and turns to the keyboard. When he's finished, when he's punched out maybe 2,500 words in four hours as he did with an Isiah Thomas story, Berkow edits it thoroughly, polishing it up and checking the spelling. Then he looks into his notebook again to make sure he didn't miss anything and to swap the exact quotes for the ones he had gotten close or paraphrased in his first draft. By the time he's done with one more edit, everything he wanted to use is in the story, and all the facts and quotes are exactly as they were in his notes.

When he wrote a many-layered, award-winning feature on the life and hard times of Hall of Fame pitcher Ferguson Jenkins, Berkow sat down at 8 A.M. on a Saturday and finished at 1 P.M.—nearly 5,000 words in five hours.

"I wrote in almost a heat," Berkow said. "It was just so dramatic."

Enterprise and investigative sports stories differ from features by exploring subjects, themes, or trends in broader formats—perhaps one long story, a succession of smaller stories over a period of weeks or months, or a three-day or five-day series, accompanied by sidebars, graphics, photos, and lists. They often involve extensive research through public records and searches for people who would rather not be quoted and may be downright hostile. They take doggedness and skill in using the Internet and library resources. They tell readers why things happened the way they did and what the impact has been. They go way beyond games, sometimes looking at questionable or illegal behavior that might have gone unnoticed.

Enterprise reporting involves digging around and beneath the surface to give readers a full view of a subject, as the AP did in two series on illegal sports gambling throughout the country and on campuses. They were series that involved several reporters researching public records and polls and conducting interviews with the FBI, police, bookmakers, gamblers, money launderers, lawyers, treatment centers, educators, athletes, coaches, and investigators from the pro leagues and the NCAA.

Investigative stories are somewhat different. They seek to break and make the news and follow it

up afterward, as the *Saint Paul* (Minnesota) *Pioneer Press* did when it found widespread academic fraud in the University of Minnesota's basketball program.

These are the kinds of stories that are showcased on the front pages of sports sections or, frequently, on the front pages of newspapers. They are high-impact stories that may lead to changes in the law, cause someone to lose a job, or affect policy in a sport. The credibility of the story, the writer, and the newspaper is at stake in every line.

Solid enterprise and investigative reporting require all the attributes of good journalism: knowledge, intelligence, judgment, perseverance, patience, interviewing savvy, research skills, storytelling, and writing talent. But they go beyond that to include a certain perceptiveness about situations that allows the writer to look at people and events in a unique way.

"The word I always twin with enterprise is *idea*," says the *Los Angeles Times*'s Bill Dwyre. "The stories that win at the APSE for enterprise are the ones with the good ideas going in. Execution is a major part of it. But if you've

Arizona Diamondbacks' Jay Bell is tagged out at home plate by New York Mets' catcher Mike Piazza in the fourth inning, Saturday, Aug. 26, 2000, in New York. Bell tried to score from third base on a sacrifice fly by Luis Gonzalez. (AP Photo/Mark Lennihan)

got a great idea, you'll have a passion for executing it."

In all stories, but especially in features and enterprise pieces that dig deeper, Dwyre says he watches out for the credibility of the sources, the holes that aren't filled, the questions that are begged.

Enterprise and investigative reporters can't resort to wiretaps like the police, but they do their detective work armed with other powerful resources: the federal Freedom of Information Act, state and county records, utility company files, reverse telephone directories, computer databases, and other elements of computer-aided research.

With tools like that, reporters can get information on such things as: college athletic budgets;

Crowds of Chicago White Sox fans vie for slugger Frank Thomas' autograph on Tuesday, June 20, 2000, at Comiskey Park in Chicago prior to the Sox' game against the Cleveland Indians. Although Tuesday's crowd was down from Monday's sellout of the park, the Sox have seen crowds increase in step with their improved record, which is currently the best in major league baseball.
(AP Photo/Ted S. Waren)

incomes of coaches; compliance with Title IX requirements for equality of male and female programs; phone records for coaches and recruiters; unauthorized use of state funds in recruiting; distribution of tickets to coaches, players, businesses, and alumni; and the addresses of athletes.

Investigative Reporters and Editors Inc. publishes the very useful *Reporter's Handbook,* organizes regional and national conferences, provides other services to reporters and editors, and seeks to maintain high professional standards in investigative reporting. The organization's Web site (www.ire.org) offers a database of reporter contacts, links, and other resources for specific beats.

Investigative Report

In an article for the *IRE Journal, St. Paul Pioneer Press* sports editor Emilio Garcia-Ruiz described the work and care that went into his newspaper's award-winning series on the University of Minnesota basketball program and the impact the series had. The process, from start to finish, was an example of first-rate investigative journalism:

> When the *St. Paul Pioneer Press* first learned that members of the University of Minnesota basketball team might be guilty of academic fraud, the newspaper set one goal for itself: Only evidence that school and NCAA investigators could not refute would appear in print.
>
> Without that sort of proof, there would be no story. Too many newspaper investigative pieces into alleged NCAA violations ultimately fizzle out. Either the school does an internal investigation that finds nothing, or the NCAA hands down what amounts to a meaningless wrist slap.
>
> So for more than three months, reporter George Dohrmann set out to find irrefutable proof of academic fraud. That meant that although his reporting could have led to publishing dozens of other possible allegations, he had to stay the course.
>
> The result was a two-story package on March 10, 1999, that detailed how almost two dozen basketball players had their course work done for them by an academic counseling office manager who later became a tutor. But the far more significant result was that the school's subsequent, nine-month, $1.5 million investigation backed up almost every major point of the first story. And heads rolled.
>
> - Four players were immediately suspended from the NCAA tournament.
> - The school self-imposed a ban on postseason play for (the next) season and put itself on probation for an undetermined length.
> - Coach Clem Haskins was dumped, albeit with a $1.5 million contract buyout.
> - It was revealed that 18 players over five years had committed fraud or NCAA violations.
> - Five athletic department officials, including the athletic director and the vice president

for athletics and student development, were told their contracts would not be renewed when they expired this year.

What made this story different from others?

Patience.

Early in his probe, in late November, Dohrmann acquired a copy of a letter from the school to the NCAA self-reporting a violation by Jan Gangelhoff, the academic counseling office manager who later became a tutor.

The letter was vague. It did not specify the violation Gangelhoff committed or give any hint of its scope. But it was news. The newspaper could have reported it as such.

Instead, the newspaper decided to continue digging.

Gangelhoff, at first, said she had no idea why the letter was sent and denied doing anything wrong. But Dohrmann stayed in touch with her and continued working other sources, who soon suggested that Gangelhoff might know more than she was letting on.

For two months, Dohrmann stayed in touch with Gangelhoff until one day she finally admitted that she had done course work. But she offered no proof. And

under the newspaper's guidelines, the word of one former tutor wasn't enough.

It wasn't until weeks later that Dohrmann, pressing Gangelhoff for proof, finally struck gold. Gangelhoff said she had done the course work on her computer and offered to allow Dohrmann to download the material so he could examine it.

The hundreds of examples of the course work that Dohrmann received on March 1 proved daunting. First, all the pieces had to be read, catalogued and cross-checked. The latter effort proved critical when matching passages were found in different papers. The duplication and other grammatical and spelling errors shared by the papers indicated the work had indeed been done by one person.

But how could the newspaper be certain the course work was legitimate?

Again, nothing would be published until the proof was irrefutable. Dohrmann flew to North Dakota and Indianapolis to interview two former players. Both confirmed Gangelhoff's admission. Two other sports writers interviewed former players who also said Gangelhoff did work for them.

All that remained now was contacting the school for comment. Unfortunately, all that hard work took time and the basketball season was almost over.

The story ran three days after Minnesota received an NCAA bid and one day before its first game against Gonzaga. The newspaper was immediately accused of damaging the home team and of timing the story to coincide with the NCAA tournament. More than 600 readers canceled their subscriptions and Minnesota Gov. Jesse Ventura called the newspaper "despicable." Attacks from former Gov. Arne Carlson continued well into 2000.

More important for the newspaper, just about every other media outfit in the state mobilized to chase the story.

With a hornet's nest stirred, Dohrmann shared the story with a newsroom-wide team, turning over source lists, phone numbers, all the documents he had acquired. He gave some of the leads he intended to pursue to colleagues and then convinced his sources to trust the paper's other reporters so they could continue his work.

The team stayed focused on academic fraud and academic fraud alone. While other media outlets went in other directions, the team set out to question something new: Did Haskins know about the fraud?

Dohrmann reported that Haskins had once written a letter of recommendation for Gangelhoff at a time he claimed to not know her. Dohrmann's tip led two other reporters, Dave Shaffer and Blake Morrison, to Alexandra Goulding, a tutor who admitted writing a player's paper and telling Haskins about it. Shaffer found past documents showing department leaders had plenty of warning that this might happen.

And finally, Shaffer badgered the university into turning over a document that proved Haskins, who had denied any knowledge of wrongdoing, had used a personal check to pay for Gangelhoff to accompany the team to Hawaii, which Gangelhoff said proved he knew what she was doing.

Newspaper staffer Rick Linsk established a spreadsheet that analyzed every aspect of the course work, by course number, by player and by any other manner deemed necessary. Shaffer worked with a Knight Ridder sister paper, *The Kansas City Star*, to borrow its exclusive database of NCAA graduation rates to analyze the rates of all schools in the Big Ten

Conference. While the NCAA publishes every school's graduation rate, it does not compare schools within a conference. Shaffer's analysis showed Minnesota was easily the worst in the Big Ten.

Kris Pope tapped his university sources to obtain players' academic information that the newspaper's legal experts would not allow in print. But the data served as critical background information that guided the team to various stories and, more importantly, away from others.

Shaffer was put in charge of one of the most difficult aspects of the story: organizing the myriad data requests that the newspaper filed with the university. They became so numerous they overwhelmed the university's public relations staff.

Judith Yates Borger handled the coverage of university administrators as the story shifted from the athletic department to the higher echelons of the school.

Three months after the story broke, with the official university investigation only half over, university president Mark Yudof waved the white flag, announcing that the *Pioneer Press'* allegations were true: The Gopher basketball team was guilty of "numerous instances" of academic cheating.

Yudof also negotiated a stunning $1.5 million buyout of Haskins' contract and fired the basketball team's academic counselor, Alonzo Newby, who had refused to speak to investigators. It was a shocking end to Haskins' 13-year run as Gophers head coach. Only two years earlier, he had taken the team to the Final Four and was named national coach of the year.

With $1.5 million paid to Haskins, $1.5 million for the investigation, and $2 million in TV payments that are expected to be forfeited because the school used ineligible players, the scandal will have cost the university $5 million.

Shortly after the first story broke, a *Good Morning America* anchor asked Gangelhoff why she had decided to come forward now. "Because," she told the country, "a *St. Paul Pioneer Press* reporter named George Dohrmann asked me to."

But while that may have been true in getting the story, it took much more to grow it.

"New Journalism"

In the late 1960s and early 1970s, the so-called New Journalism swept through newspapers and magazines, led by Tom Wolfe, Gay Talese, and the self-described heavyweight gonzo champion of the world, Hunter S. Thompson. They unleashed techniques of fiction in nonfiction features, scanned scenes or leapt into them as if they were directing cinema vérité documentaries, wielding a shaky camera and a live mike, and they wrote dazzling sports stories that lit up a whole generation of feature writers.

Sport and *Sports Illustrated* in those years shone with atmospheric writing from Al Stump and Dick Schaap to Dan Jenkins, Robert W. Creamer, and Wilfrid Sheed. Their styles could be traced back to Bill (W.C.) Heinz, Red Smith, Frank Graham, John and Ring Lardner, Damon Runyon, and the "serious" writers who visited sports at times while shaping American literature in the 20th century: John Updike, Philip Roth, Don DeLillo, Norman Mailer, Ernest Hemingway, F. Scott Fitzgerald, Jack London.

Truth be told, the roots of them all reached back to Mark Twain and Herman Melville, to Hans Christian Andersen and the Brothers Grimm, to Shakespeare and Homer, to all the great tellers of tales through time.

If sports sections have been seen for most of the past century as the toy departments of newspapers—lightweight material slapped up against the comic strips or stuck in the back as an antidote to the seriousness of the nearby business pages—they also have been the places where some of the most creative, polished writers found a home. There has been, and still is, a surfeit of flaccid or pretentious writing, but there has been, and still is, sports writing that shimmers.

Echoes of the best sports writers of the past come through in the magazine features of Frank Deford, Gary Smith, Peter Richmond, Roger Angell, David Halberstam, Leigh Montville, William Nack, Richard Ben Cramer, David Remnick.

The same echoes resound in the newspaper features of Robert Lipsyte and Ira Berkow of *The New York Times,* Tom Archdeacon of the *Dayton Daily News,* Mitch Albom of the *Detroit Free Press,* Mark Kram of the *Philadelphia Daily News,* Chris Dufresne and Steve Henson of the *Los Angeles Times,* Joe Henderson of the *Tampa Tribune,* and many others. Aspiring sports feature writers should read them all, see what makes them special, learn from them.

Jackie Robinson: The Man Who Changed Baseball and America

By HAL BOCK
AP Sports Writer

NEW YORK (AP)—There is a short wrought-iron gate and two marble benches for those who want to stay awhile.

A few steps away, a huge gray stone bearing the family name identifies the plot, and carved into the granite is one of the man's favorite sayings:

"A life is not important except in the impact it has on other lives."

It is signed in script.

Jackie Robinson.

Day after day, they still come, a steady stream of fans who navigate the narrow roads of Cypress Hills Cemetery until they reach his grave.

The cemetery, on New York City's Brooklyn-Queens border, is less than 10 miles from where Ebbets Field once stood, where the Brooklyn Dodgers played and Robinson broke baseball's color barrier 50 years ago.

Robinson's funeral cortege took the long way to get there, winding through the streets of Harlem and Bedford-Stuyvesant, the city's black neighborhoods. It was an opportunity for the people to say one final farewell to the man who changed baseball—and America.

That was not the original idea. All Jackie Robinson wanted was a job, some-thing that would pay him enough money so that he and his college sweetheart, Rachel Isum, could get married.

What he got instead was the lead role in a sociological revolution.

The Brooklyn Dodgers opened the 1947 National League season at Ebbets Field against the Boston Braves. Batting second for Brooklyn and playing first base was Jack Roosevelt Robinson, son of a sharecropper, grandson of a slave and the first black man to appear in a major league baseball game since well before the turn of the century.

Blacks had appeared in American sports before Robinson. Joe Louis was the heavyweight champion and Jack Johnson had held that crown before him. Jesse Owens won four gold medals in the 1936 Olympics.

But this was different. This was baseball, the national pastime, where integration would put a black on the field day after day, a constant reminder that the game was no longer all-white.

Branch Rickey, boss of the Dodgers, had decided to integrate baseball and chose Robinson, a marvelously skilled player. The task would not be easy. Robinson would have to silently endure every curse, every slur.

In a confrontational meeting in Rickey's office, the Dodgers' boss verbally abused Robinson with the vile words he could expect to hear on the field. It was a test to see how much the 28-year-old rookie could take.

Finally, an exasperated Robinson asked Rickey if he wanted someone who was afraid to fight back. Rickey's answer was that he wanted someone with the guts not to fight back.

The assignment began on April 15, 1947, five days after the Dodgers casually issued a two-sentence news release in the middle of an exhibition game.

"The Brooklyn Dodgers today purchased the contract of Jackie Roosevelt Robinson from the Montreal Royals. He will report immediately."

The Dodgers' players knew the day was coming, and not all of them were thrilled. There was talk during spring training of an anti-Robinson petition led by a pocket of Southern players, including Dixie Walker and Hugh Casey.

When word of it reached manager Leo Durocher, he called a midnight team meeting and chewed out the players. The revolt was crushed before it ever started, and before the year was over, the ringleaders had all been traded.

Brooklyn second baseman Eddie Stanky was less than enthusiastic about playing next to a black man.

"I want you to know something," he told Robinson on the eve of the opener. "You're on this ball club and as far as I'm concerned that makes you one of 25 players on my team. But before I play with you, I want you to know how I feel about it. I want you to know I don't like it. I want you to know I don't like you."

A famous dugout picture of the Dodgers' starting infield on opening day 1947 shows third baseman Spider Jorgensen, shortstop Pee Wee Reese, second baseman Stanky and first baseman Robinson. Stanky is the only one not smiling. The next year, Stanky was traded to Boston and Robinson, who had been a middle infielder in college, switched to second base.

Robinson arrived early for that first game and was much more relaxed than his wife, who followed with their infant son from their Manhattan hotel.

"Jack was cool and calm and ready to play," Mrs. Robinson said. "It was not a big deal for him. Whatever he felt, he kept to himself. Jack got prepared to leave with no particular discussion of what he was thinking about, no display of nerves or indication that he was worried."

On that day, before a crowd of 26,623, well under a sellout, it did not go particularly well.

The first pitcher to face Robinson was Johnny Sain, then ace of the Braves' staff. "Isn't that something?" Sain said. "Nobody knows that."

Robinson's debut was no big deal to the Braves' pitcher. "We thought he would play, but they didn't announce it until just before the game started," he said. "It was my second opening day and I was more excited that it was opening day, not who I was pitching against."

Robinson was hitless in three at-bats. He grounded to third, flied to left, hit into a double play, reached on an error on a sacrifice bunt and scored a run as Brooklyn won 5-3.

Sain saved a clipping that quotes Robinson on the opener. "It says, 'All I saw from Sain was curveballs, curves of different sizes and speeds. I wondered if I'd soon be back in Montreal.'

"I'm proud of that," Sain said. "I'm sure he was impressed."

Two days later, Robinson had his first major league hit, a bunt single. Then, in the Dodgers' next series against the New York Giants, he hit a home run. But there was trouble ahead. He slipped into an 0-for-20 slump and was about to face a major test of his endurance when Philadelphia arrived to play the Dodgers.

The manager of the Phillies was Southerner Ben Chapman and he led a fusillade of racial abuse, worse than Robinson had ever heard, worse than the darkest days of spring training in the segregated South.

- "Hey, nigger, why don't you go back to the cotton field where you belong?"
- "They're waiting for you in the jungles, black boy!"
- "Hey, snowflake, which one of the white boys' wives are you dating tonight?"

Robinson's vow of silence was facing its harshest test. The abuse from the Phillies seemed too much to take and for a tense time Robinson thought about discarding the promise, plowing into their dugout and taking on the taunters.

He called it the toughest day he had to endure in that nightmarish first season. Somehow, though, he got through it and

managed some revenge by manufacturing the game's only run in a 1-0 Dodgers victory. He singled, stole second, went to third on catcher Andy Seminick's overthrow and scored on a single.

For the next two days, the abuse increased, raining down on Robinson. Finally, one Dodger couldn't take it any more and shouted into the Phillies dugout.

"Listen, you yellow-bellied SOBs, why don't you yell at somebody who can answer back?"

The defender was Stanky, the man who had told Robinson off before the season started. Rickey was thrilled.

"Chapman did more than anybody to unite the Dodgers," he said. "When he poured out that string of unconscionable abuse he solidified and unified 30 men, not one of whom was willing to sit by and see someone kick around a man who had his hands tied behind his back. Chapman made Robinson a real member of the Dodgers."

Chapman's explanation was that this was nothing more than good, old-fashioned bench jockeying, the kind of grief any rookie could expect. He was criticized for the racial ugliness and it seemed that the affair might even cost him his job.

To save face, Chapman sent word through a friend, asking Robinson to pose for a fence-mending photograph. On the Dodgers' second trip to Philadelphia, with Rickey's blessing, the rookie and his chief tormenter met behind the batting cage. They posed together. They did not shake hands.

Robinson said later, "I have to admit that having my picture taken with that man was one of the most difficult things I had to make myself do."

Pee Wee Reese, the Dodgers' captain, was vital to Robinson's assimilation in Brooklyn.

"I knew about him," Reese said. "I knew he had played football and basketball in California. I figured he'd be good and I knew he could help us win."

And for the shortstop, that was all that mattered.

During the season, Robinson, Reese and a couple of other Dodgers sat down in the clubhouse at Wrigley Field for a game of hearts. "He was a hell of a card player," Reese said, chuckling.

Afterward, Dixie Walker and Hugh Casey, the spring training conspirators, confronted the captain. "They said, 'How can you play cards with him?' " Reese said.

He said he told Walker: " 'What's that all about? You have a black lady taking care of your kids in New York.' He said, 'It's just different.' "

There was more trouble ahead. There were rumblings about possible player strikes to protest Robinson. Al Gionfriddo, who started the season in Pittsburgh and was later a Robinson teammate, recently told ESPN that every team in the league had voted on whether to play the Dodgers.

"There were a lot of threats in the air," Mrs. Robinson said. "We'd hear rumors of organized boycotts. They were not things we could address or take too seriously. We had other things we had to manage."

The most serious talk about a walkout came from St. Louis, where the World Series champion Cardinals were angry about playing a team with a black man. This time, National League president Ford Frick stepped in.

"If you do this, you will be suspended from the league," Frick told the Cardinals. "You will be outcasts. I don't care if half the league strikes. Those who do it will encounter quick retribution. All will be suspended and I don't care if it wrecks the National League for five years. This is the United States of America and one citizen has as much right to play as another.

"The National League will go down the line with Robinson, no matter the consequences. You will find if you go through with your intentions that you will have been guilty of complete madness."

Like the Dodgers' spring training petition, the Cardinals' strike evaporated before it ever got started. And Robinson pressed on.

He was thrown at routinely, sent sprawling on a daily basis. In the first two months of the season, he was hit by pitches six times, as many times as any NL player had been hit the entire previous season.

In August, the Cardinals' Enos Slaughter, one of a fistful of Southerners who played for St. Louis, appeared to spike Robinson at first base.

The Dodgers were livid. Robinson, though, said only, "All I know is that I had my foot on the inside of the bag. I gave Slaughter plenty of room."

Then and now, Slaughter denied any wrongdoing. "I've never deliberately spiked anyone in my life," he said. "Anybody who does doesn't belong in baseball."

In Cincinnati, there were death threats against Robinson in grotesquely scrawled letters that the team gave to authorities. Teammate Gene Hermanski was so disgusted that he suggested all the Dodgers blacken their faces and wear Robinson's No. 42. "That way," he said, "they won't know who to aim at."

The Dodgers' players were typical of the time. "Most ballplayers weren't aware of the sociological changes," pitcher Ralph Branca said. "We wanted to play ball, win games and get to the World Series."

Branca helped them do that, winning 21 games at the age of 21. And as the season wore on, he realized he was watching a remarkable performance by Robinson, day-in and day-out.

"Jackie was the greatest competitor I ever saw," he said. "He didn't win. He triumphed."

One day in Chicago, Dodgers pitcher Clyde King approached Robinson. "I just asked him how he was doing," King said. "He said, 'It's tough. It's tough. It's tough.' He said it three times.

"Then he asked me how I thought it was going. I told him nobody could do it better and to hang in there. He patted me on the shoulder and walked away," King said. "It was the only time we talked about it."

Often the Dodgers were shunted from their regular lodging. Sometimes, Robinson left the team rather than disrupt the travel schedule. Always, it seemed, the Dodgers' arrival in a city created a stir because of Rickey's grand experiment.

When Brooklyn was preparing for its first trip to Philadelphia, Rickey took a call from Herb Pennock, the general manager of the Phillies, who had pitched for 22 seasons in the majors and would be inducted in the Hall of Fame the next year. Harold Parrott, one of Rickey's aides, listened on an extension and later reported the conversation.

"Just can't bring the nigger here with the rest of your team, Branch," Pennock said, according to Parrott. "We're just not ready for that sort of thing yet. We won't be able to take the field against your Brooklyn team if that boy Robinson is in uniform."

Rickey was hardly disturbed.

"Very well, Herbert," he replied. "And if we must claim the game nine to nothing, we will do that, I assure you."

There would be no forfeit, but no warm welcome, either. The Dodgers were turned away from their regular hotel and had to stay elsewhere.

Major league baseball had been an all-white operation since 1884 when Chicago manager Cap Anson caught sight of Toledo catcher Moses Fleetwood Walker, a black, warming up before an exhibition game and screamed, "Get that nigger off the field!"

But by 1959, every major league team had a black player, due in large part to Robinson's monumental effort. The Boston Red Sox were the last team to integrate, calling up infielder Pumpsie Green from the minors.

In 1957, a year after Robinson retired from baseball, he began losing weight and was diagnosed with diabetes, a disease that would eventually kill him.

Without baseball, Robinson moved to

the world of business. He became vice president in charge of personnel for Chock Full o' Nuts and spent seven years with the restaurant chain. After that, he helped start the Freedom National Bank, serving as chairman of the board of the only black-owned and -operated commercial bank in New York state.

Later, a small group of investors established the Jackie Robinson Construction Company to build housing for low- and moderate-income families.

By then, however, Robinson's health was failing. There was a mild heart attack in 1968 and another in 1970, and he began losing his eyesight. Two years later, he was honored at the World Series to mark the 25th anniversary of his move to the major leagues. Ten days after the ceremony, on Oct. 23, 1972, he died at age 53.

In his autobiography, published shortly after his death, Robinson wrote, "I had to fight hard against loneliness, abuse and the knowledge that any mistake I made would be magnified because I was the only black man out there."

He was alone at the beginning, but not at the end.

Jerry Quarry: Fight of His Life

By STEVE WILSTEIN
AP Sports Writer

HEMET, Calif. (AP)—Jerry Quarry thumps his hard belly with both fists. Smiles at the sound. Like a stone against a tree.

"Feel it," he says proudly, punching himself again and again.

He pounds big, gnarled fists into meaty palms. Right, left. Right, left. Cocks his head. Stares. Vacant blue eyes. Punch-drunk at 50. Medical name: Dementia pugilistica. Thousands of shots to the head by the best in boxing and, three years ago, the worst.

Once one of the most popular fighters in the country, a top heavyweight contender in the 1960s and '70s, he needs help shaving, showering, putting on shoes and socks. Soon, probably, diapers. His older brother James cuts meat into little pieces for him so he won't choke, has to coax him to eat anything except the Apple Cinnamon Cheerios he loves in the morning. Jerry smiles like a kid. Shuffles like an old man.

Slow, slurred speech. Random thoughts snagged on branches in a dying brain. Time blurred. Memories twisted. Voices no one else hears.

"Jerry Quarry now has the brain of an 80-year-old," says Dr. Peter Russell, a neuropsychologist who examined him recently. "Fighting aged him 30 years. He's at third-stage dementia, very similar to Alzheimer's. If he lives another 10 years, he'll be lucky."

Three Quarry brothers—Jerry, Mike and Robert—ended up brain-damaged from boxing, their lives battered by cocaine and booze, their family torn by violence and divorce.

Everything Jerry had in his career is gone. Three wives, $2.1 million in purses, $500,000 in savings. He's helpless and lost, caught feebly in the middle of a passionate family feud over his treatment.

A magnetic image of Jerry Quarry's brain three weeks ago and a CT scan last year showed the same thing: extreme cerebral atrophy, enlarged ventricles filled with fluid, a deep tunnel-like cave in the septum. His brain was rapidly shrinking, dead cells dissolving like sugar in water. Neurological tests showed severely impaired short-term memory, reasoning ability and motor skills.

"Boxers typically get a lot of repeated cerebral vascular damage," Russell said. "The small arteries and small capillaries in the brain rupture and it then leads to this kind of global atrophy of the brain."

The early signs of dementia showed up on a CT scan and in neurological tests in 1983, before his short-term memory loss and motor skills deteriorated so noticeably and before his last three fights.

Three years ago in Aurora, Colo., he thought he'd make a comeback like George Foreman, starting in a state where no license was required. Friends talked him into believing book and movie deals were in the works. He just had to get in shape and beat a couple of pugs. Instead, a clumsy club fighter whipped him in a six-round scam. A disgrace for everyone involved. The deals vanished. Broken teeth. Cuts over both eyes. Brains scrambled worse than ever. All for $1,050.

"He was missing the accolades," James says. "In making those comebacks, Jerry would walk around saying, 'I'm going to be a hero again.' To this day, if we're walking down the street or in the grocery store, he'll go tap strangers on the shoulder and ask, 'Do you follow boxing?' And if they say no, he'll ask, 'Have you ever heard of Jerry Quarry?' If they say no, he'll say, 'Well, I know you've heard of Muhammad Ali.' And they'll say yes. And he'll say, 'Well, I fought him twice, and I'm Jerry Quarry.'

"He still misses that recognition. When we take him to events and he gets the attention, his face lights up and he'll shake hands. He loves to shake hands."

Jerry, his blond hair now gray, lives with James and James' girlfriend, Brandy, in a small house on a winding hill overlooking orange groves in Hemet, halfway between Los Angeles and Palm Springs.

"Why don't we just leave?" Jerry asks.

"Where?" James responds.

"To Never-Never Land."

When James goes to work as a loan officer, Jerry, virtually in a stupor from the dementia and prescription drugs, stays home under Brandy's supervision.

"At first, all I could see is a big, 200-pound, 6-foot gorilla, and it was hard for me to accept that he was an invalid," James says. "Now I don't get upset with him. I do get a little frustrated when he walks off four or five times a day and we have to go find him. Sometimes we can't find him and we have to call the police and they bring him back."

James recently started the Jerry Quarry Foundation, sending out letters to raise money for him—Jerry's only income is $614 a month from Social Security—and to help other boxers with dementia. He removed Jerry from Dr. Russell's care and enlisted the help of the Southwest Institute for Clinical Research in Rancho Mirage, which tests new drugs for pharmaceutical companies, to examine and treat Jerry and document the severity of dementia in boxers around his age.

"He's spaced out most the time," James says. "He hallucinates. He hears voices. He cries. He gets scared. He gets confused. He can't go outside because of the medication that he's on. It makes him real sensitive to the sun. He lives in a very, very small world."

Mike's world is not much larger. He once fought for the light heavyweight title. Now he walks on his heels, swaying, losing balance. He bolts out of sleep screaming and panicking from night terrors, punches holes in walls. One eye sees up, the other down. He remembers everything about boxing, forgets things that happened a few minutes ago. Can't hold a job even as a landscaper's assistant.

He's sweet-natured and childlike at 44, still athletically built and not much above his fighting weight—"a studly 185," says his wife Ellen, a marriage and family counselor working on a doctorate in education.

"He runs, does situps," she said. "He's cut himself running, put his foot through a lead pipe and didn't know it. He came home and his foot was all bloody. He doesn't feel pain."

Less drugged and far more lucid than Jerry, Mike has the same furry edge to his speech.

"I had kind of a death wish," Mike says at his home in Diamond Bar near Los Angeles, trying to explain why he fought for 10 years after waking up in the locker room following a knockout by champion Bob Foster in 1972. "Looking back, I know I should have quit after that fight. That's when my heart went out of boxing. When a boxer is just going through the motions, that's when he gets hurt the most."

Jerry and Mike both turned to cocaine and alcohol on the downslopes of their careers, dulling their reflexes and leaving them virtually defenseless in the ring.

"The drug thing that I experienced was ignorance and rebellion," he says. "I was always in Jerry's shadow, and I rebelled against it. No matter what I did, I never surfaced on my own."

Robert, a generation apart at 32, is in jail in San Luis Obispo, trembling with symptoms of Parkinson's disease from the shots he absorbed during a mediocre, drug-filled heavyweight career.

"He got knocked out by Tommy Morrison a few years ago," James says. "Didn't spar a round and didn't run a mile. He thought that with the name Quarry he could just go out there and get paid big bucks. Well, that didn't happen."

Jerry Quarry made big bucks a few times and paid for it all with his blood. His pro record: 53-9-4; amateur, 170-13-54. Fought once with a broken hand, once with hepatitis, once with a broken back.

Thick slabs of scar tissue hang over Jerry's eyes. Jagged lines from old stitches form a map of his career's decline, long after he lost his only heavyweight title bout against Jimmy Ellis in 1968.

On the edge of the bed in James' room, he watches videotapes of the chapters of his life, grainy images that preserve the past and jog his memory. He soared at times, beating Floyd Patterson, knocking out Earnie Shavers in one round, meeting presidents and the queen of England.

"I'd do it all again, same way," he says, his speech so slow that it becomes clear only when speeded up later on a tape recorder.

Twenty-five years ago, Oct. 26, 1970, Jerry Quarry, young and blond and the top contender, earned his biggest purse, $338,000, in one blood-laced, pulsating night of racial tension in Atlanta, playing the foil for Muhammad Ali's comeback from exile. They butted heads, a gash opened above Quarry's left eye, and Ali took aim at it with fist-twisting jabs, cutting it raw and stopping him in three.

Quarry begged to fight on that night, stalked the ring in frustration when the ref signaled the end. Standing outside the arena afterward, his father and manager, Jack Quarry, a former fighter with "HARD" tattooed on the knuckles of one hand and "LUCK" tattooed on the other, advised him to quit forever.

"It's going to be another cut or another

punch in the head," Jack Quarry told him. "You've got the money now. You've got some more money out in California. Go do something. Buy ya a service station or get ya an apartment house, anything. Just get out of it."

Jack Quarry, who once drilled into his children a family motto he made up, "There's no quit in a Quarry," then walked out of his son's life. He drove up a hill one day, overwhelmed by a sense of his family out of control, and grabbed a .357-caliber Magnum pistol.

"I never hesitated," he says now from his home in Savage, Md. "I reached into the car pocket and took it out and stuck it in my mouth and pulled the trigger just like that. It didn't fire. The bullet was in there. I looked at it later. It had the hammer mark on it, but it misfired. I started saying, 'Hey, I guess the man up there has decided that I'm not going to get away that easy.' I drove back down and went on."

The breakup of the parents' marriage deeply hurt all the Quarry children, leaving them feeling betrayed and stranded even as adults. All of them now gathered around Jerry and their mother, Arwanda.

"Jerry was kind of like the spearhead, the reason to get together," Mike says. "When I was young, 13, 14, he was like a hero to me. But as I grew older, it just kind of dulled. He's still, in my estimation, the best white heavyweight of all time, with the exception of possibly (Rocky) Marciano."

As tough as Jerry was, he cut quickly in his big fights. Ali sliced him up again in a rematch. Joe Frazier slashed him even worse in their second fight, opening a gash so bad that the side of Quarry's right eyeball glistened red like a hooked fish through his torn flesh. An aged, punchy Joe Louis refereed that night in Madison Square Garden in 1974, told them to keep fighting even when they both backed off from the carnage and ringsiders roared, "Stop the fight, Joe."

Arwanda caressed her son's bloody head after that fight, urging him to quit. He wept. Retired. Changed his mind. Never listened to anyone. Started snorting cocaine and drinking. Was drunk in Hawaii when the call came to fight Ken Norton nine months later. Took another terrible beating.

Three years later in New York, almost the same scene. This time, Jerry caressed Mike's swollen, bloody face after a pounding by Mike Rossman.

"He's gonna quit, I will make him quit," Jerry said, then turned to Mike. "Say it."

"I'm gonna fight one more to go out a winner," Mike started.

"Say it," Jerry shouted.

Mike nodded with resignation but the words wouldn't come out. Jerry leaned over and kissed his brother on the neck. Mike kept fighting, off and on, for five more years.

"The fame and the fortune that came to the Quarry family broke it up, each and every one of us," says James, at 52 the oldest of Jack and Arwanda's four sons and four daughters. "This is a very dysfunctional family. There's a lot of love, but there's an awful lot of hate."

Hate and distrust are at the heart of a violent family quarrel over Jerry's care.

"Jimmy is a master manipulator," says his sister, Dianna Quarry, 49, who supports the idea of the Jerry Quarry Foundation but claims James is using Jerry to promote a self-serving book and movie script that are "packed with lies" about the family. Jerry was living with her and their mother last year a few hours away in Atascadero before going to James' house when Dianna underwent surgery.

"I'm not doing this (for Jerry) for self-serving purposes," James said. "I'm trying to do some good, probably for the first time in my life."

Old boxers and writers gathered in Los Angeles this month at a dinner to mark Jerry Quarry's induction, along with five others, in the World Boxing Hall of Fame. It is a hall without walls, a club not a shrine, a good excuse to get together for a banquet once a year and swap stories.

Jerry Quarry mumbled and rambled in his acceptance speech, couldn't sign his autograph. Wrote "J-E-R-R" on a glove and stopped. But these friends understood. He's not the only one who shuffles slowly and slurs his words.

These are the times he lives for. A night of recognition, handshakes, a long, warm standing ovation. A night to escape the solitude and confusion of dementia. A night to retreat with a fraternity of fighters into the flickering neon past.

A Brotherly Bond That Beat the Odds

By BILL PLASCHKE
Los Angeles Times

He was so small. Expecting to meet a little boy, I had just been introduced to a stick figure. His jeans hung loosely around dental-floss legs. His T-shirt swallowed the rest. I reached for his hand, and grabbed him clear up to his elbow. I had just agreed to be Andrew's "Big Brother," yet there was nothing there.

A commitment of three hours a week, each week, for the next year?

What could an active 22-year-old man possibly do with a 7-year-old shadow?

What could we ever share besides an awkward stare?

I had been told that Andrew was suffering from cystic fibrosis, a genetic predator that kills young. But an overeager counselor whispered, "Don't worry, you can't tell."

One look at Andrew's stunted growth and I could tell. One ugly cough, and I could hear.

I had just met a boy to whom I was morally bound for the next year, yet I couldn't figure out how to spend the first minute.

"So, um, what do you like?" I finally asked this little thing hugging his mother's legs.

It was then I realized I had missed something: two eyes, flickering under a mop of blond hair, eyes now bigger than all of him.

"Sports," he said, his small voice booming, and I'll remember this as long as I remember anything. "I like sports."

***

We like it, hate it, embrace it, denounce it, talk about it for hours, watch it for weekends, rip it for days. We teach with it, blame it, try fruitlessly to play it and hopelessly to understand it.

The one thing we never do, it seems, is pause and be thankful for it.

For me, for sports, this day works as well as any.

This is trying to be a Thanksgiving sports story, but not about sports as names and numbers, winners and losers.

It's about sports as language, as one of this country's most important means of communication, spanning generations, crossing economic classes, giving our diverse people something in common.

It's about how sports connected me with Andrew.

I wasn't trying to save the world. I was trying to save myself.

I had just graduated from college and was working in the swamp bureau for a newspaper in Fort Lauderdale, Fla. I was covering bowling and shuffleboard and hoping for the day when somebody would consider me good enough to cover high school football.

I lived in a one-room apartment with a bed in the wall and roaches on the ceiling. My life lacked any sense of order or importance. I figured the Big Brothers & Sisters program would give that to me.

I met Andrew Fishbein at a Christmas party in 1980.

He said he liked sports.

"What do you know?" I said. "So do I."

On our second visit, I tentatively dumped a pile of baseball cards on the floor. He dropped to his knees and ran them through his hands like money.

"Do you know how to play?" I asked.

He didn't, so I taught him a game I had learned when I was young. Soon we were sprawled out on the carpet shouting together at little pieces of cardboard, big and little now shoulder to shoulder.

And so the language of our relationship had been established, the currency set.

We played soccer as long as his clogged little lungs could handle it. We pitched baseball until it was time to go home for his medicine.

I was promoted to covering high school basketball, so he attended his first live sports event, Boyd Anderson High versus Dillard High, sitting next to me in the stands, cheering as if it were the Bulls and the Jazz.

Sports was like this for us. A language of laughter and lessons, a bridge between distant lives.

A year passed, my formal commitment to Andrew ended, but our visits continued. Sports had given us a new world—big enough for only two—that neither was willing to leave. There was always another miniature golf course to play, another pretend Super Bowl to enact with a rubber football on the scrubby field behind his townhouse.

Then in the fall of 1983, I landed a job as far from that world as Andrew thought possible. I was going to cover the Seattle Mariners, 3,500 miles away.

I still remember watching Andrew collapse in tears on the floor of his mother's townhouse. To him, I was just another man who had come and gone.

"You'll come see me, I'll stay in touch, I promise," I said quickly. "I'm covering baseball, remember?"

I'm sure he didn't believe it. I don't know if I believed it.

But it was baseball, remember? Within a year, Andrew, by then 10, had worked up the courage to fly cross-country by himself to spend long summer days with me and my wife.

Or, more to the point, to spend an afternoon with the Mariners, running the outfield during batting practice, hanging out in the clubhouse, chaperoned by an unforgettable pitcher named Roy Thomas.

As we grew older, through vastly different situations on different sides of the country, it was sports that gave us both the incentive to keep our relationship strong.

At least three times a year, we would get together, seemingly always to watch a sporting event or to hang out near a sporting event I was covering. Our reunions were, therefore, usually marked by big happy crowds, and our separations usually occurred against the echoes of cheers.

When Andrew was 13, a basketball assignment took me close enough to Florida so I could give the toast at his bar mitzvah, a wonderful celebration of manhood for a child not expected to live long past his 18th birthday.

When Andrew graduated from high school, another milestone for a kid whose lungs and digestive system were weakening by the day, he received a congratulatory phone call from Orel Hershiser.

I've never asked an athlete for anything like that before or since. But Hershiser never held it over my head because he understood the death sentence hanging over Andrew's.

Cystic fibrosis is a genetic, terminal disease affecting about 30,000 children and adults. It causes the body to produce an abnormally thick mucus that clogs the lungs and obstructs the pancreas, affecting everything from breathing to digesting.

The language of sports, of course, includes none of those words. It's about life, and I privately rejoiced that the topic of Andrew's prognosis never came up. We were too busy arguing who was better, the Dolphins or Seahawks, the Heat or Lakers.

Many times, for a boy who underwent daily chest-pounding therapies and biannual lengthy hospital stays, sports was also the language of healing.

Despondent over his situation as a freshman at the University of Florida, Andrew once swallowed enough pills to kill himself. Fortunately, a fraternity brother found him in time.

When I was finished being furious, I bought him World Series tickets, and we stayed up all night in Atlanta, talking about comebacks.

It was his first of three World Series games, one baseball All-Star game, one Super Bowl, one national college football championship, one NCAA regional basketball championship.

He has been with me everywhere from Seattle to St. Petersburg, with stops in places like Cincinnati, New Orleans, Charleston, S.C., and even Dodgertown.

He has survived two major surgeries—half of his lungs have been removed—with that same language.

Sitting at his hospital bedside, I would read him the sports pages.

Phoning his room from across the country, I would ask which game he was watching, and turn my TV to the same game, and we would shout at it together, even if he couldn't always shout.

The years passed, and I became a balding middle-ager, and the stick figure became a strong, handsome adult. Yet we stayed together until, at some point, it stopped being all about sports and started being somewhat about us.

That point was reached this fall, when I was scheduled to fly to Boston to cover what became one of the most dramatic Ryder Cup golf tournaments in history.

I flew to Jamaica instead. It was there, on a beach, that his mother and I gave Andrew away at his wedding.

On Wednesday, he flew to join me for this Thanksgiving with his new bride, Sigrid. Sure enough, the little guy has finally rumbled his way out of the corner and back up field.

Andrew is 26. He is a successful real estate agent. He undergoes countless daily therapies and painstaking hospital stays, but he works out at a gym, and is cut like a body builder.

Scientific advancements have pushed the median age of an individual with CF to 31, and here's betting he doubles it.

Today he will hug my wife as if she is his second mother, which she is. He will roll around the floor with my three children like one of their favorite uncles, which he is.

And with me? What do you think?

Today we'll watch football, eat turkey, watch football, watch more football, then fall asleep in front of the TV while watching everything replayed in 30-second video bites on the highlight show.

Some might call us lazy sports nuts. We just call ourselves brothers.

Assignments

1. Write a 1,000-word feature on a college or pro athlete, interviewing them, using file material, and contacting people who know them.

2. Pursue a theme, such as head injuries in sports, and write a 1,500-word enterprise story, talking to athletes, doctors, trainers, and so forth.

3. Construct an outline for an investigative series on college recruiting and include the names and phone numbers of people you would interview for each story. Compile clips about the subject from library and Internet sources.

Careers and Caroms

One of the first American sports writers, Bat Masterson, led an unusually adventurous life: buffalo hunter, Army scout, barroom gambler, sharpshooting sheriff in Dodge City, boxing promoter, and, for 20 years, sports writer. He keeled over on his desk in 1921 with a column in his typewriter after covering a fight for the *New York Morning Telegraph*.

Jim Murray covered Hollywood for *Time*, dining with Marilyn Monroe, playing poker with John Wayne, drinking with Humphrey Bogart, before he became, as he put it in his autobiography, "a sports writer in my journalistic dotage—which is just the right time for it."

Others have taken their own twisted roads to the sports pages. Jim Litke hopscotched from freelancer for *Rolling Stone* to sports writer at the *New Haven* (Connecticut) *Register* to a masters program in English literature to the AP Chicago bureau and back to sports as a national columnist. George Vecsey spent 10 years in sports, shifted to news as

Ted Williams, center, is applauded by Hank Aaron, left, and Willie Mays as he is introduced as a member of the Major League Baseball All-Century Team prior to Game Two of the World Series in Atlanta, Sunday, Oct. 24, 1999. (AP Photo/POOL, Ed Reinke)

Appalachia national correspondent for *The New York Times,* and returned to sports as a columnist. Mike Downey, Scott Ostler, and Joan Ryan, all superb sports columnists, crossed over to the news pages.

A journalism career can lead a writer through a variety of jobs: sports, business, general news, music, medical writing—all sorts of unforeseen subjects. Some start as writers and end up editors; some go the other way. Some leave journalism for public relations or to run the family furniture business. Some stay sports writers for life, working in one city or skipping around to a dozen.

In preparing for a sports writing career, it's not necessary to be a buffalo hunter or a connoisseur of the cinema, but it is vital to study far more than just sports and writing—even for those who plan to cover games forever. Every course I took in school, with the exception of calculus, has found a way into a story over the years.

A history course in primary source research focusing on the Sacco and Vanzetti case in the 1920s helped give me the tools to research a feature on the Jack Dempsey–Gene Tunney "Long Count Fight" and several other period pieces. Creative writing honed an appreciation for imagery and poetry and the rhythm of words. Political science, my major at the University of Wisconsin, provided insights into government and law that figured into stories on gambling, strikes, and stadiums. Statistics aided the analysis of polls and reports. Literature, philosophy, anthropology, sociology, anatomy, and astronomy all wove their way through stories.

Cramming, a highly underestimated skill, also proved helpful. Due to a fair amount of procrastinating and playing basketball instead of studying each day, I crammed for tests the night before they were given and wrote papers the day before they were due. That undoubtedly sharpened my ability to learn a lot about a subject quickly—invaluable for reporting on obscure sports at the Olympics, researching a takeout on an athlete who has died suddenly, and covering every other big story that blows in out of nowhere.

For a budding sports writer

these days, fluency in Spanish would be a tremendous advantage in covering baseball, boxing, soccer, tennis, and several other sports. French, German, Japanese, Russian: The more global sports become, the more important it is to speak other languages to get stories other reporters miss.

Every reporter has to have certain essential skills and attributes: typing fast enough to make a deadline with 1,000 words in 30 minutes and accurately enough not to make too many typos that waste time editing; taking verbatim notes in interviews and news conferences; a thorough knowledge of grammar, punctuation, spelling, syntax, and word usage; and a vocabulary broad enough to write about anything. Whether writing or editing, there are no excuses and no cutting corners when it comes to the basics.

Sports writers must go beyond that to understand the language and rules and nuances of every sport. It's not necessary to have been an athlete—most boxing writers have never fought, just as most political writers have never run for office—but it helps to have played sports on some level and have a feeling for what it's like on the court or the field. More important than any intellectual understanding or physical experience, a sports writer has to be able to grasp the games at a visceral level, genuinely relating in an intuitive, emotional way to what the athletes and fans are feeling.

"If you don't know your subject, if you don't know what you're doing, it's going to be exposed very quickly," *USA Today*'s Christine Brennan says. "Sports fans, especially, can smell a rat a mile away. You can't fake it. You can't just read a book about baseball or a press guide and memorize them. It's got to be beating inside you. You have to have a passion for sports. It's the same thing with the love of information. To be a journalist, I really think you have to have been an inquisitive child, the kind of kid who asks 'why' a lot. You have to have a real healthy sense of wanting to know things, how and why they happened. As a girl growing up, if I was sitting around the house with nothing to do, I'd pull out one of the World Book encyclopedias and just start reading it. Now we would probably go online."

New York Yankees' shortstop Derek Jeter runs toward the clubhouse under a sign quoting Yankee legend Joe DiMaggio after his team swept the Atlanta Braves in the World Series, Wednesday, Oct. 27, 1999, in New York. The Yankees defeated the Braves 4-1 in Game 4. (AP Photo/Mark Lennihan)

Aspiring sports writers, whether journalism majors or not, would do well to take every undergraduate English course available, especially short fiction writing and poetry, plus business, political science, and history as part of a broad liberal arts education. Those who want to keep growing throughout their careers should read, read, read—fiction and nonfiction, books, newspapers, and magazines, on paper or online.

Yet it takes more than an education, talent, and basic skills to become a successful sports writer. Savvy and persistence help, as do a broad base of knowledge, an absolute understanding of sports and their rules, sensitivity to people, common sense, and good judgment. Here are the recommendations of several sports editors on starting out in the business and what they are looking for:

Terry Taylor, The Associated Press: "Too many writers coming out of school think too high and too fast. The best way to break into this business is to get your start on a grass-roots level. Go to a small newspaper, cover school board meetings, high school games. That's where you can really start to develop your skills; that's where you can grow. Too many people come out of school saying, 'I want to be a foreign correspondent. I want to go to the Middle East.' Well, you have to know the basics of reporting before you go to the Middle East.

"I look for presentation, someone trying to do things a little differently, someone who grabs you with a different approach. I want someone who goes out of their way to be a craftsman. Someone who is alert and sharp. I want someone who is inquisitive, who will know what to ask, who will know the game, someone who can edit copy or write a story and enhance what we do, make our report richer and fuller and more worthwhile to put in a newspaper."

Neil Amdur, The New York Times: "My philosophy as far as recruiting people is to track them well before they come to work for *The New York Times* so they're not new to me. Liz Robbins used to do some stories for me when she was in Cornell as a student on a field hockey team. I knew who she was then and how aggressive she was. She would send me stories from St. Petersburg, and then she went to Cleveland and she applied for a job when we had an opening. I didn't think she was quite ready then. But when another opening came up, I saw her clips from the women's World Cup and the U.S. Open tennis and I said, 'Hmmm, I think she's ready.' I already knew her character and I knew her personality and I knew what I thought was her growth potential. When she came here she was ready to play."

Bill Dwyre, The Los Angeles Times: "With new writers, I'm looking for flair. That's all I look for. And I'm making sure there's no possibility that a desk editor is putting it in on the paper they're coming from. As for desk editors, I look for those who appreciate good writing, who aren't hacks, who don't tear everything apart, who have an appreciation for a writer's touch and allow the writer to stretch a little bit.

"People looking to break in should have a nice resume and offer no more than five writing samples—three is even better. They should reflect in a cover let-ter an understanding of the fact that if they get the job they are going to have to work 60 hours a week or more for the foreseeable future to get started. I recommend that they don't ever use the words 'vacation' or 'comp time' in any interview with a prospective sports editor because that's the biggest turnoff of all.

"They should understand and be able to express the fact that although they may have a fancy education, they don't know a damn thing. It all begins the day they step in the newsroom. They ought to be thrilled just to have that job. I hope people understand that this is a great business, where you can make some money and where you're not going to get bored or watch the clock. You may not become a multibillionaire, but this is a very fulfilling business and it's worth the time and the effort you put in just to get on the ladder and work your way up.

"If you have a way with the written word, somebody will find you and you'll be able to move up. Just maintain your integrity. If you're doing good work at a medium-sized paper or a small paper and it gets frustrating and takes a while, don't fear that it won't happen. If you're good, it will happen."

Dean Rock, The Dayton Daily News: "I hire for basically two things: I want to know that they have the attitude and have the intelligence. It's hard to make somebody smarter; it's hard to make somebody have a better attitude. But if you give me those two things, then I can turn a writer into a pretty solid journalist, or a better journalist if they already are solid.

"I want people who are willing to listen, who are willing to improve, who want the responsibility, with the accountability that comes with it. Basically people who are open-minded. That's the No. 1 trait. You have to be willing to change.

"People sending in resumes should follow up with a phone call. When I was in Jacksonville, we had about four openings and I had at least 200 resumes sent to me in one month. A lot of them were kids just out of college who thought they could cover the University of Florida. But I only

heard from seven people following up. That isn't to say I discarded 193 of them because of that. But one resume and one set of clips start to blend into another. Being diligent about calling is part of the application process. You have to get in touch with the editor. If they're not aggressive enough to track down a potential editor, are they going to be aggressive enough to uncover a story on the Gators beat?"

As much as sports editors look for talented writers, they also need talented copydesk editors who can save writers from themselves and make them look a lot better than they are. To many a sports editor and appreciative writer, the best copydesk editors are the MVPs of the sports department, even if they work in relative anonymity.

Editing may be a career unto itself, a step toward a writing position or a move into management. Many committed, well-educated editors proudly spend their careers on the copydesk, contributing enormously to the quality of the sports department. They share in the buzz of working on the big story on deadline, enjoy the greater stability of their shifts relative to reporters, and prefer the team atmosphere on the desk to the writer's more solitary life. Like a point guard in basketball who specializes in handing out assists, a copy editor draws satisfaction from turning a weak story into a winner.

Copydesk editors are guardians of editorial policy and style. The best pay meticulous attention to facts and sources, language and grammar. They're mindful of a story's rhythm, pace and flow, its logic, structure, scope, and detail. They respect a writer's artistry and a story's integrity, but don't hesitate to challenge either one. They catch every mistake, down to a misplaced comma, but they look at the big picture, too, finding the buried lead and analyzing stories for readability, completeness, and legal concerns. Sometimes the best move a copy editor can make is to recommend spiking a story if it doesn't back up allegations with sources and documentation.

Editors should question everything, and change nothing that doesn't need to be changed. Their greatest sin is rewriting a story and making it wrong. They

should improve stories, or let the writer improve them, if time permits, not rewrite them for the sake of rewriting. Editors should give writers the latitude to be creative and allow their distinct voices to come through, but be able to recognize the differences between artistry and affectation, between skillful discourse and rambling, self-indulgent prose.

Some editors read copy top to bottom, changing or suggesting changes along the way. Other editors go through at least three scans of stories, the first to take in the whole picture, the next to consider the outline and pace, a third to line-edit down to the finest details, and a fourth perhaps to look it all over again.

All writers have to edit themselves and, at times, others. I'm a big believer in the mumble method of editing, in which I read sentences and stories aloud to myself, kind of mumbling along the way, so that only I can hear what it's about and whether it makes any sense. By mumbling just loud enough, I can pick up the sound of sentences and the connections between them and better spot errors. It's even more effective to read a story to some-

Maracaibo, Venezuela, pitcher Ruben Mavarez reacts after the Venezuelan team won the Little League World Series championship game against Bellaire, Texas, Saturday, Aug. 26, 2000, in Williamsport, Pa. Maracaibo won 3-2. (AP Photo/Paul Vathis)

one else, particularly someone who knows very little about sports. If it works for that person, it should work for a lot of people.

The issue of length is a struggle between writers and editors at almost every paper. One of the few that doesn't set rules on length is the *Los Angeles Times.*

"One of the worst things in the world is the story that is 20 inches when it should be 80," Bill Dwyre says. "It's a terrible mistake, worse than the other way around. We try to be a literary sports section. That's a very elitist stance because we're a big paper and we can get away with it. If you're a guy at the *Dayton Daily News,* that's tough. But you should shoot for that. Sometimes you have to throw out some ads or go up two pages because we're in the word business. These are fantastic words. I don't think there's enough of that. We fall into this robotic putting out of newspapers where we don't cherish the written word as we should."

Some of the words that shouldn't be cherished are the clichés and jargon that creep too often onto the sports pages, dulling them down just when writers mean to perk them up. Hammered homers, drilled doubles, fired fastballs are a few of the offenders. Footballs thrown on a rope, Cinderella teams, hapless losers are a few more.

Writers and editors should stay on guard, too, to avoid getting suckered by athletes surreptitiously pushing products. When former baseball star Kirby Puckett discussed his glaucoma, and jockey Julie Krone talked about depression, and Olympic gold medal gymnast Bart Conner described his arthritis on *Good Morning America,* each was getting paid by pharmaceutical companies. Some of those promotional stories have dubious news value. In the cases where they are judged newsworthy, a reporter must ask whether the athlete is being paid by the manufacturer. That information should be in the story.

The sports writing racket is getting more complex as the sports pages are being read by a wider range of people. Writers and editors have to keep up with the changes, technological and social, and they have to represent the diversity of the sports and the readership.

For all the columns over the past half century that spoke of the courage of Branch Rickey and Jackie Robinson in opening up opportunities for black players in baseball, the dirty little secret of sports writing has been how few black or women writers have sat in any press boxes until relatively recently. Even as late as the 1980s, only a small number of women or minority writers cracked the line-ups of the white, male-dominated sports pages. That has changed in the past 10 years as newspapers and agencies have placed a greater emphasis on diversity:

Terry Taylor: "It used to be you would see one or two women in the press boxes. Now there are a lot more of us. It's not so odd to see women in the press box. No one stops in their tracks anymore. Isn't that wonderful?

"It's light-years from where it was when I was growing up. It's a diverse world and you have to have a diverse staff to cover it. There are plenty of opportunities out there, and there are more every year. Maybe some women think they don't stand a chance because their idea of a sports writer is a guy smoking a cigar with a little press card coming out of his hat. But I think those women are mistaken. The field is varied and wide open and it's blossoming more every year."

Christine Brennan: "Women can do anything they want to in this business. The glass ceiling, I'm sure, exists in some ways, but I think any woman or man coming into our business needs to under-stand and know that they really can go anywhere they want to and be anything they want to be. Any woman can be a sports editor. Any woman can be a sports columnist. She's got to be good. She's got to want the job. She's got to be willing to put in the hours, just like a man would. Family concerns about being a mom and raising children are big issues and can sometimes make decisions more difficult about what the woman wants to do, as well as what the newspaper or the boss would want to do. But women can do anything, and there should be nothing that's in their way."

Michael Wilbon: "The fact is that there are still only 15 or 18 black columnists in the country—that's insane. I mean, there's a couple thousand daily newspapers out there.

"There is a lot of truth to what the editors are saying, that there aren't enough black students looking to become sports writers. It's not a profession anybody black ever thinks about because they never see anyone like them doing it. I was lucky in the town I grew up in because I could read two black sports writers. But in most communities I have people come up to me and say I was the first black sports writer they had ever seen. This was just six years ago when I was 34. And I'm thinking to myself, 'I'm a pioneer in the 1990s? That doesn't make any sense.' Luckily, I hear less of it now.

"My parents didn't want me to go into journalism. It wasn't something that black parents of the previous generation thought their kids could have anything to do with. They felt they were low-paying jobs. Kids had to start off in communities that were not particularly friendly to minorities, or so they thought. There were a lot of misplaced fears about what a career in journalism was. Why did

the first black reporters go into metro? Probably because they were shoe-horned or directed into an area where they were writing about urban conditions, whatever that means. They're still under-represented on the style pages or in the business section. I don't know how many (black) foreign correspondents there are. Sports writing is probably past those sections. It's becoming an attractive thing, finally. In our culture, writing about sports wasn't something that was seen as particularly attractive or honorable. All of these things have sort of broken down over the past 20 years."

Jerry Micco: "One of the problems we have when we want to practice diversity is we take kids right out of school and put them at *The Los Angeles Times.* Boy, that's a tough crawl. I'm using the *L.A. Times* as an example. Pick your other large papers and they all fit.

"Some of these kids just flat-out aren't ready to work there. They need to work at a smaller paper, get their clips, make their errors, if you will. It's sort of like being a kid out of high school and going to major league baseball. That's a big jump. But we do it, and a lot of these kids know they can turn down a small paper because the *Washington Post* is going to get them if they're African-American or Asian or female and they show any kind of talent. I don't know if that's a good service for a young journalist. They should go where they can write every day and learn how to put a newspaper out. Where they have to do some editing and be responsible for making sure phone calls are taken and prep results are getting in the paper. Somewhere where they can get that sensitivity to a community, where when they write something people read it and care.

"At least you'll get a chance to try different things and you won't be pigeonholed. With a large paper, you're probably going to be put out into a bureau somewhere for 10 years. They're not going to put you on the main staff right away. So I tell students not to be afraid to aim a little bit small because you'll get more opportunities."

Opportunities for sports writers are opening up on the Internet, though there have been the inevitable boom-bust stories and cycles of hirings and layoffs characteristic of an infant industry undergoing rapid change. For writers willing to take a chance, a job with a sports dot-com may be an attractive alternative to newspapers, either as a way to break into sports writing or as a way to stay—doing things differently in a part of the business that is unencumbered by print deadlines and space limitations.

Most major newspapers, many smaller ones, several sports magazines, and all the national television networks operate Web sites. Many have writers and editors who work strictly in cyberspace, where more in-depth coverage may be made available than will fit on the sports pages. In addition, events like the Olympics, Wimbledon, and the U.S. Open operate their own Web sites and hire free-lance sports writers to send out stories and notes.

Here are some thoughts on the current status and future of sports writing online:

Bill Dwyre: "We went through a couple years of paranoia about how the Internet was going to take us over. I lost two of my best guys to the Internet. Some of these dot-coms are trying to build sports writing staffs starting from scratch to compete with me and other papers. I've been here 20 years, building my staff, and the *L.A. Times* had a sports section for 60 years before I got here. The framework that has been laid here is pretty tough to disrupt. ESPN.com is pretty good, but is it head-to-head competing with the *Boston Globe* or me or *The New York Times* or the *Philadelphia Inquirer* or *Dallas Morning News* or the *Chicago Tribune?* Does it do all the things that those papers do? I don't think so. I don't know how it gets there.

"There was a lot of talk in the Web world about doing away with newspapers, that in 10 years newspapers won't be what they are today and we won't even have them. I think a lot of that was just bravado. Right now, we're still the franchise."

Terry Taylor: "The Internet is a wonderful tool to help us in our job and to help us find information. . . . The bad thing about it is that there is so much that is just thrown out there with no purpose. Anything goes. I think too

many things on the Internet are done irresponsibly. The trustworthiness of the material on some Internet sites is pretty disturbing. It's kind of like, anything that sticks is OK to stick out there. People see it and think it's gospel, that it's fact, when it's not that at all. I think we're going to see more of that, and I think it's going to make us sharpen our own standards for what is responsible reporting.

"Someone coming out of school and thinking about working for an Internet sports site should examine how they report news, how they gather information, what standards they use. Do they check facts? Do they do original reporting?"

George Vecsey: "People will still be holding newspapers in their hands and reading them on the train and having them delivered to their front doorstep for a long time.

"My son is at CNNSI.com. He's smart and really knows his stuff and he should be a columnist. But he's having a good career, he's working with good journalists,

Muhammad Ali is interviewed at his training camp in Deer Lake, PA, by Steve Wilstein in 1978, shortly before Ali regained the heavyweight championship for the third time against Leon Spinks. (Photo by Robert Wilstein)

making journalistic decisions and he's using journalistic skills, editing and writing. He's also using organizing and visual skills . . . parts of his brain that I have never used.

"It's a new field and he's enthusiastic. It's another form of journalism and I don't scoff at that at all because people are getting their information from it. . . . It's a Web site, it's a television magazine, and they're not doing corny stuff or cheap shots. They know they have to be factually right.

"My son, who is 31, is already telling war stories to kids who have never worked on a newspaper. Telling them about covering high school coaches and making sure names are right and not to believe everything. He says people just out of school get hired at Web sites, not newspapers, certainly not ours.

"At *The New York Times* [Web site] they're using mostly *Times* people and we have high standards. But things get on the Web that haven't gone through the 10 layers of grind and polish the newspaper does. All the sites are going to have to deal with that in the future—have one process that is close to the same. But the fact is that the Internet is already happening. It's already a form of journalism and it will be more important as times goes on."

Women in the Locker Room

By Nancy Armour
AP Sports Writer

The first time I went into a locker room, I was an 18-year-old freshman at Marquette University. A very scared and uncomfortable 18-year-old freshman. Men's basketball wasn't my regular beat; I was just filling in over the winter break, and my experience up to that point had been limited to calling coaches and players or talking to them after practices.

Besides, there were players in that locker room I knew, who I had classes with, who I would have to see in the cafeteria every day of the year. I suppose I could have waited in the hallway until they came out, but I knew that wasn't the way I was supposed to do my job.

So I swallowed my discomfort and walked in. Sure enough, the first player I saw was a guy who'd sat behind me in a class that semester.

"Hey, there's a girl in here! What's she doing here?" he yelled.

Before I could respond, a player who'd spent some time in baseball's minor leagues before coming back to college spoke up. In a loud, clear voice, he said, "She's a reporter. Treat her like you'd treat anyone else in here."

That's exactly what they did.

Thankfully, we've come a long way from the days when women sports writers were subjected to ridicule, lewd comments, nasty remarks and worse on a regular basis simply because they were doing their jobs.

Heck, we've come a long way since 1990, when three New England Patriots were fined after Lisa Olson, then a sports writer for the Boston Herald, alleged she'd been sexually harassed in the locker room.

Professional locker rooms have been open to women for more than two decades now, and there were women in the business for decades before that. That means today's athletes and coaches have probably dealt with women reporters throughout their entire careers. We may still be a minority, but we're no longer a novelty.

Now, does this mean life is just dandy for women in sports media? Hardly.

There's still a double-standard when it comes to dealing with players and coaches outside of work. I have male colleagues who go out for dinner or drinks with players and nobody says a word. A woman sports writer does that, and her motives are questioned.

I've come across a handful of athletes who've tried to make me feel like an idiot because I've never played their sport on a competitive level, or who've made juvenile remarks to see if they could get a reaction. I've met some coaches who've been condescending.

But these incidents are isolated, and most of the people involved tend to be equal-opportunity jerks. Bob Knight makes no secret of his disdain for women sports writers, but he isn't exactly a fan of the male reporters, either. And for every Neanderthal I've come across, there are two dozen players and coaches who have treated me with the same respect and courtesy they give every other reporter.

My guess is, you could talk to women in other professions and probably find similar results. Our jobs are just a little more public.

And we are making progress. When Reggie White, the NFL's all-time sack leader, dredged up the locker room issue with an opinion piece in *The Wall Street Journal* in 1999, the response was a collective yawn. When Charlie Ward passed out copies of the article to his New York Knicks teammates, the Knicks told him in no uncertain terms that it was their locker room, not his, and they'd make the policy.

Contrary to what some people might think, women don't get into this business because they want to be groupies. I would never date an athlete and I certainly don't "ogle" them, as White claimed he'd seen some women do. In fact, I spend so much time looking at floors, ceilings and walls that I can describe to you in great detail what every clubhouse and locker room in Chicago looks like.

We're here simply because we love sports and we love to write—and most people recognize that now.

The opportunities for women in sports media are greater today than they've ever been. Gone are the days when all we could cover was "women's sports." We cover everything, from women's basketball to auto racing, figure skating to boxing. There are women columnists at some of the biggest papers in the country. The sports editor of The Associated Press, the world's largest news-gathering organization, is a woman.

And the number of women in sports media grows every year. AWSM, the Association for Women in Sports Media, has more than 600 members, and other professional organizations are popping up on what seems like a monthly basis lately.

Recently, I was in the Chicago Cubs clubhouse before a game and there were five female reporters and one male. When one of us mentioned that, the player we'd been talking to looked at us in surprise.

"You know what? I'm so used to you being here, I didn't even notice."

Playing by the Rules

Once there was a sports writer derisively dubbed "Pockets" because he covered every news conference he could get to where there was free food and stuffed his pants, jacket, and coat with hors d'oeuvres, rolls, meats, cakes, anything he could jam into his bulging pockets. He'd bring back some treats for the office and the rest for his family. An NFL draft luncheon could feed his kids for a week.

Pay wasn't too high in those days, back in the 1970s. Teams and leagues and promoters knew they could always get a crowd of sports writers if they laid out tables of food and drinks. Some went far beyond that to endear themselves to sports writers, picking up hotel bills, providing free flights, and handing out wads of tickets to events. There were boxing promoters who hired hookers for the press, and harness racing tracks that held special "sports writer nights" when they tipped the writers about which horses might win certain races. The writers made some money and the tracks got some coverage.

It was all part of the business, and it had been going on for decades, which may have accounted for why writers tended to be a bit chummier with athletes and coaches then and less hostile in print.

Things have changed, though not completely. Sports writing is still a great movable feast with fancy spreads of free food at all the major events. But the days when every baseball, football, and NBA team laid out a huge buffet for every game are long gone. Some teams serve little more than hot dogs, sodas, and coffee; some charge for meals, and some still do it the old way.

More than a few sports writers have always made it a practice to avoid the appearance of compromising their integrity by turning down offerings, whether the eatable kind or the bettable kind. They don't ask for free tickets or accept free rooms and flights because they know that, really, none of that comes free. It all comes with the unspoken understanding that the writer will pay for it with friendly coverage.

A few scandals in the business led the Associated Press Sports Editors (APSE), an organization that includes the AP and newspapers of all sizes around the country, to draft ethics guidelines. The sports editors acknowledged that guidelines can't cover every situation, and they urged using common sense and good judgment in adopting local codes:

APSE Ethics Guidelines

1. The newspaper pays its staffer's way for travel, accommodations, food and drink.
   (a) If a staffer travels on a chartered team plane, the newspaper should insist on being billed. If the team cannot issue a bill, the amount can be calculated by estimating the cost of a similar flight on a commercial airline.
   (b) When services are provided to a newspaper by a pro or college team, those teams should be reimbursed by the newspaper. This includes providing telephone, typewriter or fax service.
2. Editors and reporters should avoid taking part in outside activities or employment that might create conflicts of interest or even the appearance of a conflict.
   (a) They should not serve as an official scorer at baseball games.
   (b) They should not write for team or league media guides or other team or league publications. This has the potential of com-

promising a reporter's disinterested observations.
   (c) Staffers who appear on radio or television should understand that their first loyalty is to the paper.
3. Writers and writers' groups should adhere to APME and APSE standards. No deals, discounts or gifts are to be accepted except those of insignificant value or those available to the public.
   (a) If a gift is impossible or impractical to return, donate the gift to charity.
   (b) Do not accept free memberships or reduced fees for membership. Do not accept gratis use of facilities, such as golf courses or tennis courts unless it is used as part of doing a story for the newspaper.
   (c) Sports editors should be aware of standards of conduct of groups and professional associations to which their writers belong and the ethical standards to which those groups adhere, including areas such as corporate sponsorship from news sources it covers.
4. A newspaper should not accept free tickets, although press credentials needed for coverage and coordination are acceptable.
5. A newspaper should carefully

consider the implications of voting for all awards and all-star teams and decide if such voting creates a conflict of interest.

6. A newspaper's own ethical guidelines should be followed, and editors and reporters should be aware of standards acceptable for use of unnamed sources and verification of information obtained other than from primary news sources.

(a) Sharing and pooling of notes and quotes should be discouraged. If a reporter uses quotes gained secondhand, that should be made known to the readers. A quote could be attributed to a newspaper or to another reporter.

7. Assignments should be made on merit, without regard to race or gender.

Assignments

1. Talk with three sports writers or editors at local or national papers, asking them about their career paths, why they made career decisions, what they would recommend for someone with your interests.

2. Design your own ideal career path from first job to retirement. Write down what you would like to achieve in your career and consider what you would have to do to reach your goals.

3. Interview a retired sports writer and a retired editor, asking for their views on their careers and what suggestions they might have for you.

About the Author

Steve Wilstein is an Associated Press national sports writer and columnist based in New York. He covers sports events around the globe, including the Grand Slam of tennis, the World Series, Super Bowl, and Olympics, and has won more than 25 writing awards. In 1999, he won the AP Sports Editors award for breaking the news of Mark McGwire's use of a muscle supplement banned by most sports, which was considered the sports story of the year.

Introduction to Graphic Design Methodologies and Processes: Understanding Theory and Application

John Bowers

WILEY

John Wiley & Sons, Inc.

This book is printed on acid-free paper. ∞

Published by John Wiley & Sons, Inc., Hoboken, New Jersey
Published simultaneously in Canada

For general information about our other products and services, please contact our Customer Care Department within the United States at (800) 762-2974, outside the United States at (317) 572-3993 or fax (317) 572-4002.

Wiley also publishes its books in a variety of electronic formats. Some content that appears in print may not be available in electronic books. For more information about Wiley products, visit our web site at www.wiley.com.

Library of Congress Cataloging-in-Publication Data:

Bowers, John, 1959-
  Introduction to graphic design methodologies and processes:
  understanding theory and application/
  John Bowers.
      p. cm.
  Includes bibliographical references and index.
  ISBN 978-0-470-50435-2 (pbk),
  ISBN 978-0-470-95063-0 (ebk),
  ISBN 978-0-470-95074-6 (ebk),
  1. Design. I. Title.
  NC703.B68 2008
  760—dc22   2007051392

Printed in the United States of America

10 9 8 7 6 5 4 3 2 1